BARRON'S
WHIZ
QUIZ
SERIES

WHO ● WHAT ● WHEN ● WHERE ● WHY
In the World of

MUSIC AND ART

In the World of

MUSIC AND ART

by
Benjamin Griffith
Emeritus Graduate Dean of West Georgia College

with cartoon illustrations by
Tom Kerr
Editorial Cartoonist

All inquiries should be addressed to:
Barron's Educational Series, Inc.
250 Wireless Boulevard
Hauppauge, New York 11788

Library of Congress Catalog Card No. 91-13798

International Standard Book No. 0-8120-4479-7

Library of Congress Cataloging-in-Publication Data
Griffith, Benjamin W.
    Who, what, when, where, why—in the world of music
and art / by Benjamin Griffith; with cartoon illustrations by
Tom Kerr.
        p.   cm.—(Barron's whiz quiz series)
    ISBN 0-8120-4479-7
    1. Music—Miscellanea.   2. Art—Miscellanea.
3. Questions and answers.   I. Title.   II. Series.
ML63.G748   1991
700—dc20   91-13798
                                                       CIP

PRINTED IN THE UNITED STATES OF AMERICA
1 2 3 4   5500   9 8 7 6 5 4 3 2 1

To Betty, who makes it all worthwhile.

Contents

Introduction

"Art is long and Time is fleeting," wrote the poet Henry W. Longfellow, and "Music has charms that soothe the savage breast" (often misquoted as *beast*), penned the playwright William Congreve. So, having obtained a book of questions about art and music, you should heed the advice of these authors and get on with it if you expect to be "soothed" anytime soon.

But, alas, all may not be tranquilizing: now and then I may choose to ask a maddeningly obscure question just as a vehicle for presenting an interesting bit of information. After all, no one can be expected to know everything about the fine arts. If you remember this and bear with me, you will complete the experience with a much larger store of interesting information about painting, sculpture, architecture, classical music, opera, musical comedies, and even jazz and traditional songs. The learning can be painless, especially if you get a congenial group together for a cozy evening of questions and answers, interrupted only by laughter and perhaps a snack.

Trying to cover the highlights of so vast a subject as art and music was no easy task, as the author and his two skillful editors (Judy Makover and Diane Roth) will affirm. The time span from pictographs on a prehistoric cave wall to paintings by Picasso is quite a stretch. A similar lapse of time separates African work songs and big band jazz, liturgical chants and a Metropolitan Opera production of *Porgy and Bess*, carved bone-handled weapons and Rodin's *The Thinker*, an Egyptian pyramid and the World Trade Center, and a tune on a primitive flute and Beethoven's Ninth Symphony.

There is an almost endless store of materials for questions: each of the arts went through developing periods and changing styles, and the men and women who created art and music made important contributions along the way. Artists and musicians lead interesting lives, and some questions reflect our fascination with the distinctiveness of such geniuses. There is no way, of course, to get it all in, to cover more than a fraction of the possible questions about this important subject. And art and music *are* important, because they reflect what is most civilized, most cultured, about us human beings. "Fine art," John Ruskin wrote, "is that in which the hand, the head, and the heart of man go together." (For "man," of course, read "mankind.")

These questions are varied in type. Most of them are straightforward, but beware of the occasional outrageously tricky one. Many questions ask you to recognize the names of outstanding artists or musicians from their works or from unusual aspects of their lives. Definitions of artistic and musical terms are sometimes called for, as well as the matching of works and their creators.

So, be prepared to have a good time, enjoy a laugh here and there, and, at the same time, add to your knowledge of art and music. Good luck!

Opera: "From *Aïda* to *Zaza*"

No music lovers are so avid in their appreciation of their favorite art form as are opera lovers, or "opera buffs." And why not? Opera combines the power of music to arouse the emotions with the power of words to tell a story. Also, these dramatic works are given elaborate staging in some of the world's most beautiful buildings, and they are sung by a fascinatingly flamboyant group of singers. The great "prima donnas" of opera have sparked such public excitement that chefs have named special dishes for them and their fans have done battle in the aisles.

An incredible number of operas—more than 30,000—have been written since the idea began about 400 years ago *with a group of Florentine intellectuals who wanted to restore ancient Greek drama and set it to music. But don't be overwhelmed by the great number of operas. You can do well with the following questions if you are acquainted with the much shorter list of favorite operas, the familiar standbys of the great opera houses.*

1 In the late seventeenth century the Neapolitan school of composers introduced a new element, a way of expressing great lyric and melodic beauty through solo singing. What is the term for the pieces of solo music that allow opera singers to display their talents individually?

2 Most of the operas written by the Neapolitan school were either *opera seria* or *opera buffa*. Can you define these two types of opera?

3 This opera was first produced in Cairo, Egypt, in 1871. Though it was commissioned to mark the opening of the Suez Canal, the canal was finished in 1869, before the composer completed his task. For a three-parter, name (a) the opera, (b) its composer, and (c) its beautiful tenor aria, one of the most famous.

❹ Unique among composers, this avant-garde German genius believed that opera was not a sequence of melodies, but a complicated work of dramatic art. His masterpiece was a series of four operas based on Teutonic myths and legends. Name the composer and give the general title of this work.

❺ The composer in the previous question wrote a frequently presented opera about knighthood in King Arthur's time, and he followed it with the longest comic opera ever written; the last act alone is the length of a normal comic opera. Can you name the two works?

❻ His opera about a clown was an immediate success when introduced in Milan in 1892. Who was this composer, and what is the name of his still-popular opera?

❼ Born in Germany and trained in Italy, this composer was one of the greatest exponents of French grand opera. He moved to Paris in 1826 and began writing operas in the French style: *Robert le Diable, Les Huguenots, Le Prophète,* and *L'Africaine.* Who was he?

❽ This Italian-born composer, now a U.S. citizen, wrote an opera, *The*

Medium, that premiered at Columbia University in 1946 and opened on Broadway on May 1, 1947, with an advance sale of only $47. Because it was ignored by the public at first, the producers announced a closing date. However, word spread that the opera and its short companion piece, *The Telephone*, were good theater as well as good opera, and the show became a hit. Name the composer.

9 Can you name two other operas by the composer in the previous question?

10 Although he wrote many symphonies, concertos, and chamber works, Beethoven wrote only one opera, based on a French play by Bouilly called *Leonore*. Can you name the opera?

11 Born in England in 1872, he wrote five operas. His two best-known ones were based on great literary works: *Sir John in Love*, based on Shakespeare's great comic character Sir John Falstaff, and *The Pilgrim's Progress*, based on the allegorical work by John Bunyan. Who was he?

12 While serving in the Italian army, he wrote his first successful opera, *Zoraide di Granata*. His best works were the serious opera, *Lucia di Lammermoor*, and the *opera buffa*, *Don Pasquale*. Name him.

⑬ His opera, *Pelleas and Melisande* (1902), based on a drama by Maurice Maeterlinck, made him one of the most celebrated and controversial figures in French music. Some critics called him the prophet of the future, but others thought he was a charlatan. Do you know his name?

⑭ This opera had a lukewarm premiere in 1935. When it was revived in New York in 1942, the music critics called it a masterwork. It became the first opera by an American-born composer staged at the historic La Scala in Milan. Who was he, and what is the name of the opera?

⑮ Can you match the operas in the list on the left with the correct composers in the column on the right? Since the principal word in all these operas begins with the same letter, this test should suit you to a "T."

Operas	Composers
1. *La Traviata*	**(a)** Puccini
2. *Thaïs*	**(b)** Offenbach
3. *Il Trovatore*	**(c)** Mozart
4. *The Telephone*	**(d)** Massenet
5. *Tannhäuser*	**(e)** Berlioz
6. *Tale of a Real Man*	**(f)** Menotti
7. *Tales of Hoffmann*	**(g)** Prokofiev
8. *Tosca*	**(h)** Rossini
9. *Les Troyens*	**(i)** Verdi
10. *William Tell*	**(j)** Wagner

Identify the operas in which the following actions occur and name the composer of each.

16 A concert hall singer falls in love with Dufresne, only to learn he has a signora as well as a bambino.

17 Papageno uses a musical instrument to capture birds.

18 A witch transforms children into gingerbread figures.

19 An overweight soldier sends love letters to two of the most respected ladies of the town, Mistress Ford and Mistress Page.

20 A philosopher sells his soul to the Devil in order to obtain wealth and power.

21 Don José kills Escamillo's girlfriend with a dagger.

22 Two of the most popular operas contain music sung by groups rather than soloists. Can you name one opera with a famous sextet and one with a well-known quartet? Also, name the composer of each.

23 Born in England in 1913, this composer wrote an opera based on a short novel by Herman Melville, *Billy Budd*. It is the story of a young midshipman, almost a Christ-like figure, who was the object of obsessive hatred by the evil Claggart. Can you name the composer?

24 One of the most light-hearted of operas, this two-act *opera comique* has a text based on Shakespeare's *Much Ado About Nothing*. It is some of the composer's sunniest music, but he wrote it while suffering from an unfortunate marriage and poor health. Name the opera and the composer.

25 Amilcare Ponchielli (1834–86) is remembered for one major triumph, an opera produced at La Scala in 1876 that created a sensation. It is based on Victor Hugo's tragedy *Angelo* and features a love affair between a Genoese nobleman and a ballad singer. What is the title?

26 A powerful older Viennese musician and composer who envied the young Mozart tried to prevent the production of two of his operas. They were presented, however, to great acclaim. Can you name Mozart's rival and the two operas he tried to suppress?

27 This English composer, organist, and harpsichordist wrote operas about classical myths as well as the legends of British heroes. His best-known opera and his masterwork is *Dido and Aeneas*. Who was he?

28 This stately dance, first popular in France at the court of Louis XIV, became popular with composers as a musical form. One of the most celebrated uses of it is found in Mozart's *Don Giovanni*. Can you name this dance?

㉙ This term means literally "beautiful song." It also describes the art of singing lyrical arias in Italian opera. What is this term?

㉚ Male eunuchs with artificial female voices were popular in the eighteenth century in opera performances. What is the Italian word for this type of singer?

㉛ What is the name given to a device developed by Wagner whereby a recurrent theme identifies a character, emotion, incident, etc.?

How much do you know about famous opera singers? Test yourself with the following questions.

㉜ Regarded as the greatest Italian bass of the early twentieth century, he appeared in every opera house in the world and more than 750 times in fifty different operas at the New York Metropolitan. He is best known, however, for his singing of one special song in *South Pacific*. Can you name the singer and his song?

㉝ After her success in the role of Julietta at London's Covent Garden, she appeared there regularly until 1914, missing only the 1909 season. She was a high coloratura, famous for her portrayal of Rosina, Lucia, Gilda, and Violetta, and Saint-Saëns wrote the opera *Hélène* for her. (Hint: An ice cream dessert and a kind of toast were named for her.) Do you know her name?

❸❹ He began his operatic career in 1913 singing baritone roles, and made his "second debut," this time as a tenor, in 1918 in *Tannhäuser.* His greatest successes came in Wagnerian opera, and he sang Tristan over 200 times. Do you know his name?

❸❺ She was from Norway and had an operatic career limited to Scandinavia from 1913 to 1933. In 1934 she was offered small roles in Wagnerian operas at Bayreuth, which led to major Wagnerian roles at the Metropolitan, where in 1935 she sang Brünnhilde and Kundry for the first time. The critics called her the "greatest Wagnerian soprano of the day." Name her.

❸❻ A Greek, born in New York, she studied in Athens and made her debut in 1938. Because of her range and style, she was the first soprano since Lilli Lehmann to sing Isolde and Lucia as well as Brünnhilde and Violetta. Considered controversial, perhaps because of the dramatic intensity she brought to her roles, she withdrew from public appearances after 1964. Name her.

37 Born in Sydney, Australia, she became the resident soprano for the Royal Opera at London's Covent Garden Theatre in 1952. She is internationally famous for her role in Donizetti's *Lucia di Lammermoor*. Name her.

38 Born in Naples in 1873, he possessed one of the most beautiful tenor voices the world has ever known. He was the first true "gramophone" tenor, successfully recording from 1902 to 1920. His record of "Una furtiva lagrima" (1904) is considered one of the great operatic recordings. Who was he?

39 Known as the "Swedish Nightingale," she was so popular in Vienna that the Empress threw one of her own bouquets on the stage—an unprecedented act. P.T. Barnum, of circus fame, brought her to America. Who was she?

40 He began singing in a New York synagogue at six, made his debut at the Metropolitan in 1945, and achieved stardom a few months later as Radames in a famous broadcast version of *Aïda*, directed by Arturo Toscanini. Name him.

41 One of America's great contralto singers is an African-American, the first of her race to sing at the Metropolitan. In 1939 she was forbidden to give a concert at Washington's Constitution Hall by its owners, the Daughters of the American Revolution. Instead, she gave an open-air concert for 75,000 persons at the Lincoln Memorial. Who is she?

42 This soprano has had an outstanding career as both a singer and director. She joined the New York City Opera in 1955 and became the company's diva. After a career that included roles in the world's leading opera houses, she became general director of the New York City Opera and retired from the stage in 1980. Name her.

43 The most popular singer in the "Live From the Met" telecasts, on which he has appeared many times since the first broadcast in that series in March, 1977, is a tenor born in Modena, Italy. Can you name him?

44 At the celebration of the Bicentennial of the French Revolution in 1989, a statuesque American soprano was seen on worldwide television as she sang the "Marseillaise," wearing a flowing gown and cape in the colors of the French flag and striding dramatically at the base of the Arc de Triomphe. Who is this singer, known for her leading roles in *Aïda* and *Les Troyens*?

45 Born in Madrid, this tenor had his first big break when he sang Pinkerton in *Madame Butterfly* as an understudy. The following year he began a long association with the

Metropolitan Opera Company. A busy performer, he once sang three different lead roles in a single month (March, 1982) at the Metropolitan. Name him.

46 Although he sang frequent opera roles at Covent Garden and the Metropolitan, this Irish tenor was better known for his sell-out concerts in which he sang "Mother Macree," "Macushla," and "I Hear You Calling Me." Can you name him?

47 The greatest bass singer in opera history is generally conceded to be this Russian star, extremely tall at six feet six inches. Most opera lovers consider his portrayal of the title role in *Boris Godunov* as unparalleled. Name him.

48 A famous horn player named Franz was a bitter enemy of Wagner's music. At a rehearsal, conducted by Wagner, he angrily left the orchestra pit, refusing to play such "outlandish music." Ironically, his son Richard was an avid fan of Wagner's music as well as the composer of two great operas: *Elektra* and *Der Rosenkavalier*. Name this composer.

49 This Czechoslovakian composer was dedicated to developing the musical life of his native land. The most significant of his nationalistic works was the comic folk opera *The Bartered Bride* (1866). It is filled with national dances and folklike melodies. Who was this composer?

50 One composer was known for recycling his old operas into new ones, in effect plagiarizing himself. His best-loved opera, about a Spanish barber, has an overture which he also used in two of his previous operas, and he lifted five major numbers from five other operas. Name the composer and the opera.

51 There is another much-loved opera based on the same story by Beaumarchais, and dealing with the same Spanish barber. Can you give the title and composer?

52 The only surviving opera written by this versatile composer is an excellent spectacle that includes a famous love song, "My Heart at Your Sweet Voice." The hero has his locks shorn and becomes powerless. What is the name of the opera, and who was the composer?

53 This composer of grand opera began by composing marches for the town band in Busseto, Italy. His fellow citizens raised funds to send him to the Milan Conservatory, but his application was rejected. Composing without instruction, he achieved success with his third opera *Nabucco*. Name him.

54 The composer in the previous question led a long and productive life, writing one of his masterpieces, his only comedy, when he was eighty. Can you name this opera about a humorous Shakespearean character?

55 This opera, based on a poem by Pushkin, is set in Saint Petersburg in 1815. It opens in a garden, where two daughters await the arrival of two young men. It includes a famous waltz, which is played at a birthday ball. Can you name the composer and the opera?

56 Another Russian composer, whose father was the leading basso of the Saint Petersburg opera, is best known for such precedent-shattering orchestral works as *Le sacre du printemps* and *L'oiseau de feu*. He also wrote a one-act comic opera, an adaptation of a folk tale about a cock and a fox. Can you name the composer and his opera?

57 One of the most popular of all operas was produced three months before the composer's death. Its temporary failure probably hastened its creator's death, but later productions were acclaimed. One of its best-known songs, *Habanera*, is from a Spanish folk dance melody. Who was the composer, and what is the name of the opera?

58 This composer is remembered for only one opera, *La Juive* (*The Jewess*), which gave Caruso one of his famous roles. In fact, Caruso was stricken with his fatal illness while onstage in this opera. Who was the composer?

59 One of the great natural geniuses of music, this composer worked at incredible speed. He wrote the overture to his greatest opera, *Don Giovanni* the night before the premiere. The musicians played it from sight, the ink still wet on the pages. Name him.

60 Some of the world's architectural gems are buildings in which opera is presented. Match these famous opera houses with the cities in which they are located.

Opera House	**City**
1. Staatsoper	**(a)** London
2. Opera Comique	**(b)** Munich
3. Royal Opera House (also known as Covent Garden)	**(c)** Vienna
4. National Theatre (Bavarian State Opera)	**(d)** Paris
5. Metropolitan	**(e)** New York
6. Fenice Theatre	**(f)** Milan
7. Court Theater (Drittningholm Palace)	**(g)** Stockholm
8. Grand Theatre	**(h)** Venice
9. San Carlo Opera House	**(i)** Geneva
10. La Scala	**(j)** Naples

61 Called the father of German Romantic Opera, his concept of writing authentically German opera, as distinguished from the Italian products, led him to write *Der Freischütz*. It was a sensation, coming at the time of a wave of nationalism in Germany. His last opera was *Oberon*. Who was he?

Identify these characters from famous operas by their actions. Also name the operas and composers.

62 She is a high priestess of the Druids, in prehistoric Britain, who cuts the sacred mistletoe.

63 He is the chief of a village comedy troupe who murders a young peasant named Silvio with a dagger.

64 This soldier in the Spanish army mortally wounds Don Carlo and then throws himself off a cliff as a group of monks arrive singing a mass.

65 He is a notorious seducer of women who comes to Seville by night and enters the apartments of Anna.

66 She conceals an outlaw named Johnson in the attic, and Rance, the sheriff, discovers him by the dripping blood.

❻❼ The daughter of a Brahman priest in India, she sings the aria "Where goes the maiden straying," accompanied by bells.

❻❽ This naval lieutenant tries to contract a temporary marriage with a beautiful Asian girl.

❻❾ Lionel is desperately in love with her and steals a rose, promising to return it if she will sing for him. She sings "The Last Rose of Summer."

❼⓪ He is a minstrel knight who escapes from the real world in order to enjoy sensual pleasures with Venus, the goddess of love.

❼❶ This fisherman is exonerated of the charge of murder, but the townspeople view him with suspicion.

❼❷ One measure of the interest in opera in the United States is the number of opera companies in the country with an annual budget of a half million dollars or more. Would you guess that the number is (a) twenty (b) fifty, or (c) seventy-five?

❼❸ The leading composer and pianist in the "ragtime" era of 1895–1920 wrote an opera, which he produced at his own expense for a single performance in Harlem in 1911. It has since been performed widely. Name the composer and his opera.

74 An Italian composer who identified with Mussolini and the Fascist regime in Italy inaugurated a new style of opera called *Verisimo,* or naturalism. His most popular opera was *Cavalleria Rusticana,* first produced in Rome in 1890. Name him.

75 Television host David Frost describes this opera in contemporary language: "There's these four aging hippies, see, living in a garret—a poet, a painter, a writer, and an amiable bum who is a philosopher. They can't pay the rent, but there's always someone worse off than yourself. Sure enough, when Rudolpho is left alone, a girl appears, cold and hungry, with the rather flimsy excuse about getting a light for her candle." Can you name the opera and the composer?

76 Try another, though Mr. Frost had nothing to do with this one. "There was this big dame, you know, who had been asleep on a rock in a, like, magic spell. A guy name Siegfried wakes her up, and they marry and go live in a cave." Name the opera and composer.

77 One more, for the road: "There is going to be this big party, see, with everybody wearing costumes like on Halloween. Later, a guy named Reinhart threatens to kill his wife because she has fallen for the Governor. She begs off, and he decides then to kill the Governor." Name the opera and composer.

78 She was the first woman conductor at the New York Metropolitan and is well known as a producer of opera. The first opera she staged was Vaughan Williams's *Riders to the Sea* at Tanglewood. She founded the Boston opera in 1957 and has been its director since. Who is she?

Answers

① *The "aria," shortened from what Alessandro Scarlatti called the* aria de capo. *Arias allowed the projection of melodic expressiveness hitherto unknown.*

② *If you are a real "opera buff," you know that* opera buffa *is comic opera and* opera seria *is the serious variety.*

③ *(a)* Aïda, *(b) Giuseppe Verdi (1813–1901), and (c)* "Celeste Aïda."

④ *Richard Wagner (1813–83). The four operas are known collectively as* Der Ring des Nibelungen *(1876), or sometimes just* The Ring. *The four long operas are individually named* Das Rheingold, Die Walküre, Siegfried, *and* Götterdämmerung.

⑤ Tristan und Isolde *and the comic opera* Die Meistersinger.

⑥ *Ruggiero Leoncavallo (1858–1919), who wrote the beloved* I Pagliacci.

This short opera is so often performed as a double bill with Cavalleria Rusticana *that opera lovers refer to the two as "Cav and Pag."*

⑦ *A German who made good in France, Giacomo Meyerbeer (1791–1864).*

⑧ *Gian Carlo Menotti (1911–   ), who is also the founder of the Spoleto Festival in Charleston.*

⑨ *Menotti's other works include* Amelia Goes to the Ball, The Old Maid and the Thief, The Island God, The Consul, Amahl and the Night Visitors, *and* The Saint of Bleecker Street.

⑩ Fidelio, *Op. 72 (1805), the story of the unjust imprisonment of Florestan and his ultimate release because of the devotion of his wife, Leonore.*

⑪ *Ralph Vaughan Williams (1872–1958), who also wrote nine symphonies, a piano concerto, and a violin concerto.*

⑫ *Gaetano Donizetti (1797–1848). During the period when he was writing his most successful compositions, he suffered from hallucinations and depressions and was confined to a mental hospital for the three years before his death.*

⑬ *Claude Debussy (1862–1918). He tried to prevent the opening of the opera in 1902, saying that the work "has become almost an enemy alien to me" and was being presented "against my will."*

⑭ *George Gershwin (1898–1937), who composed the beloved folk opera,* Porgy and Bess.

⑮ *1(i), 2(d), 3(i), 4(f), 5(j), 6(g), 7(b), 8(a), 9(e), 10(h).*

⑯ Zaza, *by Ruggiero Leoncavallo (1858–1919).*

⑰ The Magic Flute, *by Wolfgang Amadeus Mozart (1756–91).*

⑱ Hansel and Gretel, *by Engelbert Humperdinck (1854–1921).*

⑲ Falstaff, *by Giuseppe Verdi (1813–1901).*

⑳ Faust, *by Charles Gounod (1818–93).*

㉑ Carmen, *by Georges Bizet (1838–75).*

㉒ *The sextet from* Lucia Di Lammermoor, *by Gaetano Donizetti (1798–1848), and the quartet from* Rigoletto, *by Giuseppe Verdi (1813–1901).*

㉓ *Benjamin Britten (1913–76). He also wrote other operas:* Peter Grimes, The Rape of Lucretia, Albert Herring, *and* A Midsummer Night's Dream.

㉔ Beatrice and Benedict, by *Hector Berlioz (1803–69), who also wrote the operas* Benvenuto Cellini *and* Les Troyens.

㉕ La Gioconda.

㉖ *Antonio Salieri (1750–1825). He tried to suppress* The Abduction from the Seraglio *and* The Marriage of Figaro.

㉗ *Henry Purcell (1659–95). He also wrote the operas* King Arthur *and* The Fairy Queen.

㉘ *Minuet. Verdi also used the form in* Rigoletto.

㉙ *Bel canto.*

㉚ *Castrato.*

㉛ *Leitmotiv.*

㉜ *Ezio Pinza (1892–1957), who was applauded for his singing of "Some Enchanted Evening" in the film and stage version of the Rodgers and Hammerstein show.*

㉝ *Dame Nellie Melba (1861–1931).*

㉞ *Lauritz Melchior (1890–1973). He appeared in several motion pictures, including* Luxury Liner *(1947) and* The Stars Are Singing *(1952).*

㉟ *Kirsten Flagstad (1895–1962). She had a voice of great power and radiance, superbly projected.*

③⑥ *Maria Callas (1923–77), who had special dramatic and musical talents that lent themselves to revivals of works by Rossini, Bellini, and Donizetti for which she was the perfect heroine.*

③⑦ *Dame Joan Sutherland (1926–), who is married to the conductor Richard Bonyng.*

③⑧ *Enrico Caruso (1873–1921), said to have earned enormous sums in the 1920s from the royalties of his recordings.*

③⑨ *Jenny Lind (1820–87). She had a remarkable purity of tone and a phenomenal range.*

④⑩ *The famous American tenor, Richard Tucker (1915–75).*

④① *An important forerunner, Marian Anderson (1902–).*

④② *Beverly Sills (1929–).*

④③ *The Italian tenor, Luciano Pavarotti (1935–).*

④④ *Jessye Norman (1945–).*

④⑤ *The Spanish tenor, Placido Domingo (1941–).*

④⑥ *John McCormack (1884–1948). So popular was he on the concert stage that during the 1914–18 period, he appeared only nine times in operas, but gave 400 concerts.*

④⑦ *The great Russian basso, Feodor Chaliapin (1873–1938).*

④⑧ *Richard Strauss (1864–1949), who also wrote* Salome, *a one-act opera that outraged the morals and sensibilities of a generation of opera lovers.*

④⑨ *Bedrich Smetana (1824–84). He also wrote the opera* Dalibor *(1868), whose principal character is the hero of a Bohemian revolt against tyranny.*

⑤⓪ *Gioacchino Rossini (1792–1868), the composer of* The Barber of Seville.

⑤① *Mozart's* The Marriage of Figaro, *based on the same source as Rossini's opera, also features the barber Figaro.*

⑤② Samson and Delila *(1877), the work of Camille Saint-Saëns (1835–1921).*

⑤③ *Giuseppe Verdi (1813–1901), who also wrote the beloved* Rigoletto, La Traviata, *and* Aïda.

⑤④ *The comic opera,* Falstaff, *written by Verdi in 1893.*

⑤⑤ *Peter Ilyich Tchaikovsky (1840–93), who wrote* Eugene Onegin *(1879).*

Significant revivals in Europe and America in the 1940s and 1950s have given this opera the high stature it deserves. The waltz is untitled, but is played in the opera at a ball celebrating Tatiana's birthday.

⑤⑥ *Igor Stravinsky (1882–1971). He wrote the opera* Renard *as well as* Le Rossignal, Maura, *and* The Rake's Progress.

⑤⑦ *Georges Bizet (1838–75), composer of* Carmen.

⑤⑧ *Jacques François Elias Halévy (1799–1862).*

⑤⑨ *Wolfgang Amadeus Mozart (1756–91).*

⑥⓪ *1(c), 2(d), 3(a), 4(b), 5(e), 6(h), 7(g), 8(i), 9(j), 10(f).*

⑥① *Karl Maria Von Weber (1786–1826), now better known for the overtures of his operas.*

⑥② *Norma, from the opera* Norma, *by Vincenzo Bellini (1801–35).*

⑥③ *Canio, in* I Pagliacci, *by Ruggiero Leoncavallo (1858–1919).*

⑥④ *Don Alvaro, in* La Forza Del Destino, *by Giuseppe Verdi (1813–1901).*

⑥⑤ *Don Juan (or Don Giovanni), from* Don Giovanni, *by Wolfgang Amadeus Mozart (1756–91).*

⑥⑥ *Minnie in* The Girl of the Golden West, *by Giacomo Puccini (1858–1924).*

⑥⑦ *Lakme, who sings "The Bell Song," a favorite of opera lovers everywhere, in the opera* Lakme, *by Léo Delibes (1836–91).*

⑥⑧ *Lieutenant Pinkerton, in* Madame Butterfly, *by Giacomo Puccini (1858–1924).*

⑥⑨ *Harriet, known to some farmers as Martha, in the opera* Martha, *by Friedrich von Flotow (1812–83).*

⑦⓪ *Tannhäuser, from the opera* Tannhäuser, *by Richard Wagner (1813–83).*

⑦① *Peter Grimes, in the opera* Peter Grimes *by Benjamin Britten (1913–76).*

⑦② *The answer is (c). According to the current edition of* The World Almanac and Book of Facts, *in July of 1990 there were seventy-five opera companies in the United States with a half-million dollar budget.*

⑦③ *Scott Joplin (1868–1917). The opera was* Tremonisha.

⑦④ *Pietro Mascagni (1863–1945), who became wealthy as the result of the success of his opera, but died in poverty and disrepute.*

⑦⑤ La Bohème *by Giacomo Puccini (1858–1924)*.

⑦⑥ Die Gotterdammerung *(The Twilight of the Gods), by Richard Wagner (1813–83)*.

⑦⑦ The Masked Ball, *by Giuseppe Verdi (1813–1901)*.

⑦⑧ *Boston's Sarah Caldwell (1924–   ), who conducts the orchestra for most of her productions.*

Songs and Singers

Musicologists tend to believe that all songs—indeed, all music—comes ultimately from folk songs. The songs that people sing while working, drinking, recording some local event, or expressing feelings such as love or patriotism are very important. In the dim past these songs were written by the "folks": anonymous untrained composers. Later, trained composers took these tunes and reworked them into songs as varied as national anthems or Tin Pan Alley ballads. You may be in for some surprises in this section, which will test your knowledge of everything from the oldest known "round song" to recent hit records.

❶ For an easy beginning, here are questions about a song played at most American sports events: our national anthem. (a) In what war did Francis Scott Key observe the "rockets' red glare" of battle, and (b) from what song did Key take his melody?

❷ In 1832 the Reverend Samuel Francis Smith wrote the words to "America." He found the tune in a collection of German songs and was struck by its patriotic possibilities, although unaware that the same tune was used in the British national anthem. Name the song that is dear to Britons.

❸ Two favorite hymns, "Onward Christian Soldiers" and "Brightly Gleams Our Banner," were written by a composer who, along with a collaborator, became famous for comic operas. Who was he?

❹ General Ulysses S. Grant, who became the eighteenth president of the United States, once said, "I know only two tunes; one of them is 'Yankee Doodle,' and the other isn't." Although he may not have had an ear for music, perhaps the President did know the meaning of the line from that song: "Stuck a feather in his cap and called it macaroni." Do you?

❺ Others, unlike President Grant, may have musical ears too sensitive to listen to amateur singers. Supply the missing rhyme to this couplet by Samuel Taylor Coleridge:

Swans sing before they die—'twere no bad thing
Should certain persons die before they _____.

6 This will be an easy one for you, especially if you know some foreign languages. Try matching these popular songs with their country of origin.

Song	Country
1. "Eili, Eili"	(a) Canada
2. "Dark Eyes (O Chichornia)"	(b) France
3. "Mien Nierlandsch Bloed"	(c) Czechoslovakia
4. "Marseillaise"	(d) Belgium
5. "Hamidji March"	(e) Israel
6. "Kimgayo"	(f) Japan
7. "Battle Hymn of the Hussites"	(g) Russia
8. "Brabançonne"	(h) Holland
9. "La Paloma"	(i) Spain
10. "The Maple Leaf Forever"	(j) Turkey

7 Determined to write a patriotic melody, this composer wrote the "Emperor's Hymn," soon adopted as the Austrian national anthem. Later, it was used throughout Germany. Who was the composer, and what is the version of the song that came to symbolize German imperialism?

8 One of the most famous compositions of all time is an English song about the change of seasons. It is the oldest piece of harmonized music still sung today and the oldest known "round" song. Can you name it?

9 Two of the most popular "rounds" of today deal with a trio of handicapped rodents and a type of waterfront activity. Can you name the songs? For extra credit, define "round" songs.

10 In the colonial times in America one of the favorite types of songs was printed on single sheets to be sold. They usually dealt with a current news event, set to a familiar tune. What were these sheets called?

11 In the late 1950s and 1960s a popular type of music was folksinging. When groups gathered to sing, they gave the event a special name, which was also used as the name of a televised folk song program. What was it?

12 During this time when folksinging was in vogue, both traditional songs and newly written protest songs were popular. Match these singers with the songs they made famous.

Songs	**Singers**
1. "Scarlet Ribbons"	**(a)** Burl Ives
2. "Bridge Over Troubled Water"	**(b)** The Weavers
3. "Like a Rolling Stone"	**(c)** Peter, Paul, and Mary
4. "Blue-Tailed Fly"	**(d)** Judy Collins
5. "I Am Woman"	**(e)** Simon and Garfunkel
6. "Kisses Sweeter Than Wine"	**(f)** Bob Dylan
7. "Where Have All the Flowers Gone?"	**(g)** Helen Reddy
8. "Society's Child"	**(h)** Harry Belafonte
9. "If I Had a Hammer"	**(i)** Janis Ian
10. "Turn, Turn, Turn"	**(j)** Pete Seeger

⓭ A popular folksinger of the 1960s was a full-blooded Cree Indian whose songs often protested the treatment of her people. Name her.

⓮ This enormously popular singer, called "The King" by his adoring fans, was born in 1935 and died in 1977. His home in Memphis, Tennessee—Graceland—has become a type of shrine to his memory. Who was he, and can you name at least five of his hit songs?

⓯ Two of America's favorite folk songs are "Goodnight, Irene" and "Rock Island Line," made popular by a singer named Huddie Ledbetter. He is better known by his nickname. What was it?

16 In the 1840s a type of musical entertainment appeared with dancers, musicians, singers, and comedians made up in blackface. One troupe, originally known as the Virginia Minstrels, were later named for the originator of this type of show. What was the group then called?

17 A singer who starred on Broadway and in the movies often used minstrel-show makeup in his act. Another trademark was kneeling as he sang, a practice that began when he knelt one night to relieve pressure on an ingrown toenail. Who was this singer-actor who starred in the first movie with sound, *The Jazz Singer* (1927)?

18 One of America's greatest composers of popular songs was linked closely with the minstrel shows. A nonsense song about traveling west with a banjo on a certain part of one's anatomy was his first hit, for which he was paid $100. Name the song and the composer.

19 The composer in the preceding question had a major success with a song in 1851, selling 40,000 copies of the sheet music the first year, rising to 130,000 by 1854. He originally mentioned the Pedee River in the song, but changed to another river that he thought had a more musical sound. Name the song.

㉔ One of the most endur-
ing type of American songs is African-American in
origin and is usually sung by choral groups. Typical
of such songs are "Deep River" and "Swing Low,
Sweet Chariot." What are these songs called?

㉑ One important type of
folk music is the blues. In 1914 the most widely
performed blues song of them all was published.
The composer has a street named for him in Manhattan, but the song only mentions a city in the
Midwest. Name the composer, and name his blues
song.

㉒ What comedian, known
for his bulging eyes, had a tremendous hit with an
Irving Berlin song, which sold a million copies of
the record and the sheet music in the first year?
For extra credit, name the song.

㉓ Which Ziegfeld Follies
star, known for such songs as "Second Hand Rose"
and "My Man," was portrayed by Barbra Streisand
in the Broadway show *Funny Girl?*

㉔ Americans love non-
sense songs, and one of the best remembered was
written in 1923, after the songwriters (Frank Silver
and Irving Cohn) overheard a Greek fruit peddler
deliver a classic line to a customer inquiring about
fruit. Name it.

㉕ In 1929 a young singer
and bandleader brought his band, The Connecticut

Yankees, to New York and was greeted by huge bands of squealing youngsters not to be equaled until Frank Sinatra later appeared on the scene. Name him and his famous theme song.

26 Another crooner who became famous as a movie star has been called "the groaner," "the Gentile cantor," and "the boo-boo-boo-boo-boo man." Name him.

27 One of the most popular Civil War songs among the Union troops was the unofficial national anthem of the abolitionists. The name in the title is coincidentally the same as that of a man who led an antislavery attack on Harper's ferry, but it actually refers to a sergeant in the Massachusetts Volunteers. Name the song.

28 The tune in the preceding question was based on a camp meeting song popular with black congregations, "Say, Brothers Will You Meet Us?" A young lady poet and suffragette was asked to put more dignified words to the tune. Can you name her and the still-popular hymn she wrote?

29 If there is one tune known all over the world, it is *Malbrough* or *Malbrouck*. This melody was sung in the twelfth and thirteenth centuries by the Crusaders and Arabs in Palestine. Many know the tune as *He's a Jolly Good Fellow*. Do you know the titles of two other versions of this song?

❸⓿ Jack Yellen (1894–1991), a Polish-American songwriter who voted Republican, wrote the favorite campaign song for the Democratic party. If you've watched that party's national conventions on television, you've heard it. Name the song.

❸❶ A song by Henry Clay Work (1832–91), written during the last days of the Civil War, was resented by the Southern troops, but it has long been popular. Its melody was later used to promote woman's suffrage, Prohibition, the Populist party, and more recently, Princeton's football teams. Name it.

❸❷ One kind of folk song was very important to sailors who worked at hoisting sails, raising anchors, and pulling bowlines. What is the name given to such songs as "Haul Away, Joe," "Blow the Man Down," and "The Drunken Sailor"?

❸❸ This French composer wrote about 200 songs with piano accompaniment, but he is best known for one religious song, popular at weddings, which he adapted from the melody of a Bach prelude. Name the composer and the song.

❸❹ A famous French philosopher is said to have written the well-known song, "Twinkle, Twinkle, Little Star," in a dream. Who was he?

35 For almost twenty-five years Beethoven nursed the desire to set to music a great poetic ode about the brotherhood of man by a fellow German. In his last symphony, the Ninth (1824), he succeeded in incorporating a choral ode into the symphonic form. What was the name of the poem he set to music, and who was the poet?

36 In June, 1962, a twenty-one-year-old singer-composer who also believed passionately in tolerance for all races was interviewed about his new song, which was having a strong effect on the Civil Rights movement. He said, "There ain't too much I can say about this song except that the answer is blowing in the wind. . . Man, it's in the wind—and it's blowing in the wind." Know the composer? I'm sure you can guess the title.

37 Another song, which became the unofficial theme song of the Civil Rights movement in the 1960s, was adapted from an old hymn of the same title. Name it.

38 In Mexico, Americans are sometimes referred to by the name "gringos." What does this have to do with songs? It is generally believed that the word "gringo" was coined by Mexicans who heard American troops in the Mexican-American War in the 1840s singing their favorite song. Can you name it? (You'll want to kick yourself—or me—when you see the answer.)

39 One American folk-singer and composer is best known for his "Dust Bowl Ballads," which came out of the anguish and poverty of the Great Depression of the 1930s. His son Arlo is also a prominent folksinger. Can you name him?

40 The first major song hit to come out of World War II combined a kind of religious fervor with the war effort. The words and music were by Frank Loesser, a New Yorker who was to become one of Hollywood's and Broadway's most successful lyricists. Name the song.

41 Irving Berlin (1888– 1989) would probably not have dared predict such a phenomenal success for himself even "if I live to be a hundred" (and he did). He wrote three songs that have earned extraordinary royalties, in part because two of them are seasonal. Name them.

42 Bing Crosby introduced the song in a 1934 movie called *She Loves Me Not*, but Jack Benny, with his infamous violin, took over the song as his own. Name it.

43 The song that won the Oscar for 1944 (sung in the movie *Going My Way*) had a humble beginning. Lyricist Johnny Burke, hearing Bing Crosby scolding one of his children severely for behaving "like a mule," wrote the funny and inspirational song Bing sang in the movie. Name it.

44 A song in the most popular movie musical of all time also has animals in it and is sung by some children and their governess. The song begins "Doe, a deer...." For a three-parter, (a) who was the governess, (b) what was she trying to teach the children, and (c) who wrote the song?

45 One of the most beloved of all motion picture songs was introduced by Ukelele Ike in the *Hollywood Review of 1929*. It became a national sensation when it was sung in a movie by a dancer in a downpour. Name the song and the dancer.

46 The best-selling single record ever cut by the Columbia Records Company was made by a cowboy singer. (Hint: It's a song about an animal with a physical abnormality that is laughed at by his peers, but later becomes a great asset.) Name the singer and the song.

47 One ingredient always present in a folk ballad is a story. In 1958 a trio of folksingers gained popularity with a story song about a mountain man who was "bound to die" for his crime. Name the trio and the song.

48 Ready for a Matching Question? Try to match the following titles of popular songs with the singers who made them their special trademarks. It will help if you are well over forty. The baby boomers will get their chance later.

Song Title	Singer
1. "How Much Is That Doggy in the Window?"	**(a)** Ella Fitzgerald
2. "Mule Train"	**(b)** Frank Sinatra
3. "Blue-Tailed Fly"	**(c)** Jo Stafford
4. "Fly Me to the Moon"	**(d)** Tony Bennett
5. "Tired"	**(e)** Burl Ives
6. "You Ain't Nothin' but a Hound Dog"	**(f)** Patti Page
7. "I Left My Heart in San Francisco"	**(g)** Rosemary Clooney
8. "A-Tisket, A-Tasket"	**(h)** Frankie Laine
9. "Come-on-a My House"	**(i)** Pearl Bailey
10. "You Belong to Me"	**(j)** Elvis Presley

49 Of all the folk ballads that sing of sad events, the favorite is one that was mentioned in Samuel Pepys's seventeenth-century diary and became a hit record for Joan Baez. It tells about Sweet William's dying of love. Name it.

50 One of the first songs written expressly for television was like a folk song and was about a legendary character who was called the "king of the wild frontier" in the song. Name it.

51 A valuable barometer of popular song successes was a radio program that began on April 20, 1935, and continued for twenty-eight years (the last three on television). It featured the ten most popular songs each week. Can you name it?

52 Nearly every schoolchild has heard this merry Italian song that was written in 1880 to celebrate the opening of cable car service to the top of Mount Vesuvius. Name it.

53 A fiddle tune that was immensely popular during the early nineteenth century, this has been called the "most American of all tunes." An endless string of verses has been written to it, enough to last as long as the fiddler holds out. Name this song with a type of poultry in the title.

54 Almost everyone sings this song at least once a year. A Scottish poet wrote some of the verses and copied the others from the singing of an old man, believing it to be the first time the ancient song had been written down. Name the poet and the song.

55 For this Matching Question, readers who were teenagers in the fifties have an advantage. Match the performers on the right with their hit songs on the left.

Song	**Performer**
1. "Don't Be Cruel"	**(a)** Jerry Lee Lewis
2. "Diana"	**(b)** Bobby Darin
3. "Blueberry Hill"	**(c)** Buddy Holly
4. "Roll Over Beethoven"	**(d)** Fats Domino
5. "Rock Around the Clock"	**(e)** Everly Brothers
6. "Splish, Splash"	**(f)** Ricky Nelson
7. "Great Balls of Fire"	**(g)** Elvis Presley
8. "Wake Up Little Susie"	**(h)** Paul Anka
9. "I'm Walkin'"	**(i)** Chuck Berry
10. "Peggy Sue"	**(j)** Bill Haley

56 Whether we know French or not, most us can sing "Alouette," a Canadian voyageur song. Do you know which bird is referred to in the title?

57 One of the most famous of all railroad songs tells of the wreck that took the life of a "brave engineer" on the Illinois Central line. Name him.

58 The Western folk song, "Whoopee Ti-Yi-Yo," as well as many other cowboy songs, mentions "dogies." What is a "dogie"?

59 This song, written in 1878 by the Hebrew poet Nephtali Herz Imber and set to music by Samuel Cohen, was taken up by the Palestine colonists and became the anthem of the Zionist movement, organized in 1897. Name it.

60 Have the last two sets of Matching Questions missed your age group completely? Don't despair; try putting these titles with the performers that made hit records of them in the sixties and seventies.

Song	Performer
1. "Satisfaction"	(a) Led Zeppelin
2. "I'm Henry the Eighth, I Am!"	(b) Beatles
3. "Don't Go Breaking My Heart"	(c) The Who
4. "Eight Miles High"	(d) Dave Clark Five
5. "People Are Strange"	(e) Petula Clark
6. "Glad All Over"	(f) Rolling Stones
7. "I Want to Hold Your Hand"	(g) Elton John
8. "Happy Jack"	(h) Herman's Hermits
9. "Good Times, Bad Times"	(i) The Byrds
10. "Downtown"	(j) The Doors

61 No singer has been identified so completely with one team of songwriters as Dionne Warwick. Name the composer and lyricist of her hit songs.

62 Can you name two of the songs this team wrote for Ms. Warwick?

63 One beautiful night in 1929 this composer was sitting on the "spooning wall" at the University of Indiana, musing about a girl he had once loved and lost. A melody came to him which has become one of America's all-time classics. Name the composer and his song.

64 He gathered an armful of Oscars for songs and background music for the movies in the 1960s and had his first big hit with a song Andy Williams sang as the screen credits rolled for *Breakfast at Tiffany's* (1961). Name the composer, the song, and the lyricist.

65 They became a sensation when they arrived in New York from England and appeared on the Ed Sullivan TV show in 1964. Can you name the group, the members of the group, and at least five of their hits?

Answers

① *(a) The War of 1812, which lasted well into 1814, when this song was written to describe a British attack on Fort McHenry,*

near Baltimore. (b) The melody was from "To Ana-
creon in Heaven," which Key had used nine years
earlier when he wrote a patriotic song called "When
the Warrior Returns." (Try singing these four words
to the first notes of "The Star Spangled Banner.")

② "God Save the King."
The Reverend Mr. Smith was not quite as confused
and tone deaf as the English lady in the anonymous
limerick:
There was an old person of Tring,
Who, when somebody asked her to sing,
Replied, "Ain't it odd?
But I cannot tell "God
Save the Weasel" from "Pop Goes the King."

③ Sir Arthur Sullivan
(1842–1900), of Gilbert and Sullivan fame, who was
knighted by Queen Victoria.

④ A "macaroni" was an
eighteenth-century English fop who loved fancy clothes
and putting feathers in his cap. A feather in your cap
if you got it right!

⑤ "Sing."

⑥ 1(e), 2(g), 3(h), 4(b),
5(j), 6(f), 7(c), 8(d), 9(i), 10(j)

⑦ Franz Joseph Haydn
(1732–1809), who actually used a melody from a
Croatian folk song when he wrote the song that became "Deutschland, Deutschland über Alles."

47

⑧ *"Sumer is icumen in." The manuscript of this song in the British Museum is dated about 1240.*

⑨ *"Three Blind Mice" and "Row, Row, Row Your Boat." A "round" is a short song, with different groups singing in unison, but beginning at different time intervals.*

⑩ *Broadsides.*

⑪ *Hootenanny.* Pete Seeger led a group of singers in a famous live concert recording, Hootenanny at Carnegie Hall.

⑫ *1(h), 2(e), 3(f), 4(a), 5(g), 6(b), 7(j), 8(i), 9(c), 10(d).*

⑬ *The folksinger is Buffy Sainte-Marie (1942–   ).*

⑭ *Elvis Presley, of course. Some of his hits include "Blue Suede Shoes," "Love Me Tender," "The Wonder of You," "Memories," and "Jailhouse Rock."*

⑮ *"Leadbelly," who spent many of his years in a Texas prison and was later discovered by John and Allan Lomax, important folk song collectors.*

⑯ *The group known as Christy's Minstrels, named for Edwin P. Christy (1815–62), who introduced the song "Farewell, Ladies" as his group's concluding number. It is still sung as "Goodnight, Ladies."*

(17) *Al Jolson (1886–1950), who was born in Saint Petersburg, Russia.*

(18) *"Oh! Susannah" is the song, Stephen Collins Foster (1826–64) was the composer.*

(19) *"Old Folks at Home" is the title. Some may think the title is "Way Down Upon the Swanee River."*

(20) *Spirituals.*

(21) *W.C. Handy, "The St. Louis Blues." Handy also wrote "The Memphis Blues," "The Harlem Blues," and "The East of St. Louis Blues" among others.*

(22) *Eddie Cantor (1892–1964), who is also remembered for the songs "Ida, Sweet as Apple Cider" and "My Blue Heaven" (in which he interpolated lines about his five daughters). The hit song was "You'd Be Surprised."*

(23) *Fanny Brice. She was singing in a shabby burlesque house in 1910 when Florenz Ziegfeld discovered her and brought her to Broadway.*

(24) *This popular nonsense song is, of course, "Yes, We Have No Bananas."*

(25) *Rudy Vallee (1901–86), "I'm Just a Vagabond Lover."*

(26) *The crooning movie star was Bing Crosby (1903–77).*

㉗ *"John Brown's Body."*

㉘ *Julia Ward Howe wrote "The Battle Hymn of the Republic" in 1861. The opening line "Mine Eyes Have Seen the Glory of the Coming of the Lord" came to her, she said, in her sleep.*

㉙ *"We Won't Go Home Until Morning" and "The Bear Went Over the Mountain" are two other versions. The original French words, which refer to the Duke of Marlborough, Napolean's adversary at Waterloo, begin: "Marlborough s'en va-t-en guerre" ("Marlborough is going to war").*

㉚ *"Happy Days Are Here Again" (1929). Other songs of Mr. Yellen include "Down By the O-Hi-O" (1920), "I Wonder What's Become of Sally" (1924), and "Are You Having Any Fun?" (1939).*

㉛ *This old but still well-known melody is "Marching Through Georgia."*

㉜ *Chanteys. To be more technical, chanteys for brief tasks were called "short hauls," and those for longer ones, "halliards."*

㉝ *Charles Gounod (1818–93), who wrote the song "Ave Maria."*

㉞ *Jean-Jacques Rousseau (1712–78). Although he was not a trained composer, he produced the popular opera* Le Devin du Village (The Village Sorcerer), *which contains this song.*

㉟ *"Ode to Joy" by Friedrich Schiller (1759–1805), a poet and dramatist. This poem contained Beethoven's ideal of the brotherhood of all mankind. He believed passionately in the equality of man.*

㊱ *Bob Dylan (1941–), who was born Robert Zimmerman, wrote the song "Blowing in the Wind," which referred to changing attitudes toward racial injustice.*

㊲ *"We Shall Overcome."*

㊳ *"Green Grow the Lilacs," a song that goes back to seventeenth-century Scotland. You may have to pronounce "green grow" with a Latin accent to make this work.*

㊴ *Folk composer Woodrow Wilson ("Woody") Guthrie (1912–67), who inspired a whole generation of folksingers with his Victor album* Dust Bowl Ballads. *His best-known song is "This Land Is Your Land."*

㊵ *"Praise the Lord and Pass the Ammunition," written immediately after the Pearl Harbor attack. It was an instant success.*

㊶ *"God Bless America" (written in 1918 and first popular in 1938), "Easter Parade" (1933), and "White Christmas" (1942).*

㊷ *"Love in Bloom."*

㊸ *"Swinging on a Star." Burke added a pig, a fish, and other animals to the song.*

㊹ *(a) Julie Andrews, playing the role of Maria Von Trapp, (b) The musical scale, and (c) Richard Rodgers (1902–1979) and Oscar Hammerstein (1895–1960).*

㊺ *"Singing in the Rain," sung by Gene Kelly.*

㊻ *Gene Autry, "Rudolph the Red-Nosed Reindeer."*

㊼ *The group was the Kingston Trio. The song is "Tom Dooley."*

㊽ *1(f), 2(h), 3(e), 4(b), 5(i), 6(j), 7(d), 8(a), 9(g), 10(c).*

㊾ *"Barbara Allen."*

㊿ *"The Ballad of Davy Crockett" (1954), about the famous frontiersman, soldier, and congressman.*

(51) *"Your Hit Parade." Some of America's greatest popular singers appeared on the show, including Dick Haymes, the Andrews Sisters, Margaret Whiting, Ginny Sims, Doris Day, Frank Sinatra, Lawrence Tibbett, Dinah Shore, and Giselle McKenzie.*

(52) *"Funiculi, Funicula." Such a cable car in Europe is called a "funicular,"*

but if I had included that word in the question, it would have been too easy!

(53) *"Turkey in the Straw."*

(54) *Robert Burns (1759–96), "Auld Lang Syne" (which refers to the "days of old, long since").*

(55) *1(g), 2(h), 3(d), 4(i), 5(j), 6(b), 7(a), 8(e), 9(f), 10(c)*

(56) *The skylark, which would not care for the action threatened by the song: "I will pluck you. I will pluck your (1) head, (2) neck, (3) wings, (4) back, and (6) tail."*

(57) *Casey Jones.*

(58) *"Dogies" are stunted calves that have been abandoned by their mothers, sad to relate.*

(59) *The stirring, emotional "Hatikvah" (The Hope).*

(60) *1(f), 2(h), 3(g), 4(i), 5(j), 6(d), 7(b), 8(c), 9(a), 10(e)*

(61) *The composer is Burt Bacharach (1928–); the lyricist is Hal David (1921–).*

(62) *Choose from "Walk on By," "I Say a Little Prayer," "Alfie," and "Do You Know the Way to San Jose?"*

(63) *Hoagy Carmichael (1899–1981), "Star Dust."*

(64) *Henry Mancini (1924–), "Moon River," and Johnny Mercer (1909–76).*

(65) *The Beatles (John Lennon, Paul McCartney, Ringo Starr, and George Harrison). Some of their hits were "Hey Jude," "Let It Be," "A Hard Day's Night," "Yellow Submarine," and "Yesterday."*

Musical Comedies and Operettas

Beginning in the 1920s Broadway set a high standard for the musical theater. Most of Europe's best composers of operettas emigrated to America to be a part of the magic. At the same time, American musical comedies, written by a brilliant array of composers and lyricists, were loved and imitated throughout the world. In the 1970s musical comedies of a new type were developed in the theaters of London and Paris, moving to New York with great acclaim. Let's see what you know about music written to be performed behind the footlights.

❶ A clever British comic playwright, who also wrote sophisticated songs for musical reviews, surprised the opening night audience in London's West End with a brilliant Strauss-like operetta, set in Vienna. It was called *Bittersweet* and contained a lovely waltz, "I'll See You Again," and the song "Zigeuner." Name him.

❷ An American composer, called the "March King," was also determined to be successful with his operettas. Some of his early attempts were *Our Flirtation* (1880), *The Smugglers* (1882), and *Desirée* (1884). His only success was an operetta about the Viceroy of Peru, who was disguised as a rebel bandit. Give the title and composer.

❸ In order to write this operetta, W.S. Gilbert (1836–1911) and Arthur S. Sullivan (1842–1900) went to Portsmouth to inspect the H.M.S. *Victory*. Gilbert made sketches of the ship and riggings in order to design the set, and he also designed the uniforms. Name the operetta.

❹ Speaking of Gilbert and Sullivan, can you name four other operettas they wrote?

❺ After writing two mildly successful operettas, this composer scored his first hit with *Babes in Toyland* (1903), with its exciting "March of the Toys" and spectacular effects. Who was he?

6 Referring to the composer in the preceding question, name three more of his popular operettas.

7 He is considered by many to be "the" American songwriter and is said to have written more than a thousand songs. "I wrote more failures than any other songwriter on earth," he said, "because I write more songs than anyone else." He also wrote scores for more than twenty Broadway musicals, beginning with *Watch Your Step* (1914) and ending with *Mr. President* (1962). For a two-parter: (a) who was he, and (b) can you name three of his successful musicals?

8 Rudolph Friml (1879–1972) is one of America's most distinguished composers of operettas. His best score is generally said to be one that included the songs "Only a Rose" and "Love Me Tonight." The story is based on the romanticized exploits of the French poet François Villon. What is the title?

9 A classic American operetta, first produced in 1927, has the characters Magnolia, Gaylord, Julie, Joe, Captain Andy, and Queenie. For a two-parter: (a) name the operetta, and (b) name the composer.

10 In a popular operetta that ran for 509 performances when it opened in 1928 in New York, there is a song "Softly, as in a Morning Sunrise." The humorist Ring Lardner wrote that he *did* wonder about the morning sunrise, "as distinguished from the late afternoon or evening sunrise." Who was the composer and in what show is this song featured? For extra credit, can you name two other popular songs from this show?

⑪ This operetta by the composer mentioned above was based on a romantic German novella *Alt-Heidelberg*. Some of its best numbers include a drinking song ("Come, Boys"), "Deep in My Heart," and "Golden Days." Can you name the operetta?

⑫ The composer in the preceding question made two early successes in America with adaptations of European operettas, both with "time" in their titles. One of them became a great film success with Jeanette MacDonald and Nelson Eddy in 1937. It featured a love song, "Will You Remember?" Can you name these two adapted operettas?

⑬ This Viennese waltz king was encouraged by his wife Henrietta to enter a sphere of music more ambitious than the waltz: the operetta. He was already well known for *The Blue Danube Waltz* and *Tales of Vienna Woods*. Who was the composer, and what were the names of his two masterworks of the operetta form?

⑭ In 1905 a Viennese operetta was produced that used the waltz for romantic, psychological, and plot purposes, and it was danced as much as sung. It was the beginning of a new wave of modern operettas. Name the composer and the operetta.

⑮ This German composer of some of the greatest musicals of the twentieth century had the advantage of working with some of the best librettists and lyricists: Bertolt Brecht, Moss Hart, and Ogden Nash. He also wrote a musical version of Elmer Rice's *Street Scene*. Name the composer and the three works in which he collaborated with the above-mentioned writers.

⑯ The composer Stephen Sondheim has a dark side. He has written a musical about a London barber who murders his customers and allows his landlady to make meat pies of their remains. He also wrote a recent musical in which Grimm's fairy tales became very grim indeed. What is the title of these two shows?

⑰ Sondheim is well known for his many successful musicals that are not sinister. Try naming three of them.

⑱ The great Leonard Bernstein (1918–90) collaborated with Sondheim on a celebrated musical that mixed *Romeo and Juliet* with New York street gangs. Name it.

⑲ One of the most successful pair of collaborators for the musical theater, these Americans first became prominent for a musical review called *The Garrick Gaieties*, which opened on Broadway in 1925. They later went on to write many musicals. For a three-part question: (a) who were they, (b) which one wrote the music, and (c) can you name four of their shows?

20 This brash Broadway show about gamblers and Salvation Army workers opens with a number entitled "A Fugue for Tinhorns." Can you name the show and the composer of the musical score?

21 In 1956 a show opened on Broadway that was billed as a "comic operetta." Not considered likely to be a box office success, it was based on a 1759 satire by Voltaire. Though it ran only seventy-three performances in its original production, it is considered the composer's greatest musical work for the stage. Can you name the composer and the comic operetta?

22 What is the musical term for operettas that are based on preexisting music, usually by a single composer? (Hint: The term is the same as the Italian word for pie and pudding.)

23 Can you name the composer and lyricist of a Broadway show that featured a circus spectacle, complete with elephants?

24 A landmark Broadway musical opened on March 31, 1943, to unexpected triumph. It featured a great deal of dancing, some of it similar to Western square dancing, but it also had a dream ballet choreographed by Agnes de Mille. For this two-parter: (a) who were the composer and lyricist, and (b) what is the title?

25 This duo's most popular musical (which became one of the most successful filmed musicals of all time) was set in Austria and was based on a true story of a spunky governess and her adopted family. Name the show.

26 In what Broadway musical is a story by the Roman playwright Plautus retold for modern audiences?

27 Ready for a series of Matching Questions? First, can you match the Rodgers and Hammerstein songs on the left with the musical comedies in which they are featured?

Song	**Musical**
1. "Bali Ha'i"	(a) *Sound of Music*
2. "Getting to Know You"	(b) *Carousel*
3. "Oh, What a Beautiful Morning"	(c) *The King and I*
4. "You'll Never Walk Alone"	(d) *South Pacific*
5. "Climb Every Mountain"	(e) *Oklahoma*

28 Now match the songs at the left with the Gilbert and Sullivan operettas on the right.

Song	Operetta
1. "I've Got a Little List"	(a) *Pirates of Penzance*
2. "When I Was a Lad"	(b) *The Mikado*
3. "When I, Good Friends, Was Called to the Bar"	(c) *Ruddigore*
4. "The Slave of Duty"	(d) *Trial by Jury*
5. "My Eyes Are Fully Open to My Awful Situation"	(e) *H.M.S. Pinafore*

29 The songs at the left are all found in the American operettas listed on the right. Can you match them? For extra credit, who was the composer?

Song	Operetta
1. "Gypsy Love Song"	(a) *Sweethearts*
2. "Italian Street Song"	(b) *Mlle. Modiste*
3. "Every Lover Must Meet His Fate"	(c) *The Red Mill*
4. "Every Day Is Ladies Day With Me"	(d) *The Fortune Teller*
5. "I Want What I Want When I Want It"	(e) *Naughty Marietta*

㉚ Match the popular song on the left with the musical comedy in which it was featured.

Song	Musical
1. "Papa, Won't You Dance with Me?"	(a) *Mame*
2. "If He Walked Into My Life"	(b) *Pal Joey*
3. "The Party's Over"	(c) *High Button Shoes*
4. "Diamonds Are a Girl's Best Friend"	(d) *Hair*
5. "I've Grown Accustomed to Her Face"	(e) *Gentlemen Prefer Blondes*
6. "Bewitched"	(f) *My Fair Lady*
7. "The Girl That I Marry"	(g) *Sweet Charity*
8. "Everything's Coming Up Roses"	(h) *Gypsy*
9. "If My Friends Could see Me Now"	(i) *Annie Get Your Gun*
10. "Let the Sunshine In"	(j) *Bells Are Ringing*

㉛ This operetta that featured a Canadian Northwest Mounted policeman was tremendously popular when it appeared in the fall of 1924. It followed a large number of films on a similar subject—between 1921 and 1923 there were no less than forty feature films with Canadian mountie plots! For a two-parter: (a) who was the composer, and (b) what is the title of his operetta?

32 The first Broadway musical to win the Pulitzer Prize dealt humorously with American politics. Do you know the title and the brother team that wrote the score and lyrics?

33 This colossal hit in New York and London, based on a play by George Bernard Shaw, reflects that author's interest in linguistics and in the class struggle. Can you name this show and its creators?

34 This musical comedy by the same pair mentioned in the previous question, was set in Scotland and featured a love affair that linked the twentieth and eighteenth centuries. Give the title.

35 Still another hit show by the duo mentioned in the two preceding questions features the characters of King Arthur, Queen Guenevere, Sir Lancelot, and Morgan LeFay. Among its lasting songs are "If Ever I Would Leave You" and "How to Handle a Woman." Name the show.

36 This greatest of all ballad operas was the 1728 sensation of London. It featured the lovely Polly Peachum and the heroic highwayman Macheath (who would become "Mack the Knife" in Kurt Weill's *Three Penny Opera*, a twentieth-century version). Who was the author, and what was the title?

37 This most popular of Gilbert and Sullivan operettas makes its attack on British institutions with an oriental cast and setting. Though the Lord High Executioner seems determined to behead someone, it is a comedy about death in which no one dies. What is the title?

38 A musical comedy about the gold rush has two attractive songs that deal with nature: "They Call the Wind Maria" and "I Talk to the Trees." Do you know the title and writers of this musical?

39 A Broadway musical that has become one of the most popular of shows in the operetta theaters of Eastern Europe was written by a composer of light, sophisticated songs. The plot concerns a Shakespearean company that is acting in *The Taming of the Shrew*. Who is the composer, and what is the name of this show?

40 This Broadway show, with music by Stephen Sondheim, was based on an Ingmar Bergman film, *Smiles of a Summer Night*. It is a somewhat somber show despite the fact that its composer wrote every song in a variant of three-quarter time. Can you name the show and its most popular song?

41 This Broadway show, which opened in 1936, was hailed as a theatrical breakthrough because it used ballet for the first time as an integral part of the plot. The choreographer George Balanchine, working with his first musical comedy material, was a major contributor. The show was revived in New York and London in the 1980s and again the remarkable ballet, "Slaughter on Tenth Avenue," was a hit. What was the title?

42 In the spring of 1991 a musical show opened on Broadway with the largest advance sale in history. It was the first show to break the $100 barrier for the best seats. What is the title of this show with a primarily Asian cast? Who were the writers?

43 In 1966 very few fans of Broadway shows believed it possible that a musical comedy could be written about Nazi Germany. Director Hal Prince believed in the show, however, and used the music and lyrics of an obscure duo and the talents of a diminutive singer-dancer to mold a hit show. Can you name the show and its writers? For extra credit, who was the male star?

44 This musical comedy, with music and lyrics by one person, was based on a French play and presented by a primarily male cast, some wearing female costumes. One of its best-known songs is "We Are What We Are." Name the composer and his show.

45 Can you name two other hugely successful musicals by the composer mentioned above?

46 A perennial, often-revived musical that opened in 1934 has most of the action on a ship. One of its most popular songs is "I Get a Kick Out of You." Who wrote it, and what is the title?

47 This musical by one of today's most successful composers is based on a book of poems by Thomas Stearns Eliot, one of the twentieth century's most important poets and literary critics. Its best-loved song is entitled "Memories." Can you name the show and the composer?

48 This brilliant musical was developed in France, and in translation it has become a long-running hit in London and New York. Based on a book by Victor Hugo, it is the story of a good man who has run afoul of the legal system. Can you name the show and its writers?

49 The longest-running musical comedy on Broadway is primarily a dance review interspersed with highly personal monologues by dancers trying out for a show. The director of the show, who also conceived and choreographed it, is given the primary credit for its success. Can you name him and his famous show?

50 This musical comedy, based on one of the great novels of American literature, tells the story of a boy and a runaway slave. The music and lyrics were written by a newcomer to Broadway who was previously known for his comic popular songs. Who is he, and what is the title of the musical?

51 Set in 1905 in a village in Czarist Russia, this Broadway musical has a main character who talks to God as he milks his cows. Can you name: (a) the show, (b) the composer and lyricist, and (c) the main character?

52 What musical holds the record for the greatest number of consecutive performances in theatrical history? (Hint: The featured song is "Try to Remember.")

53 Based on the life of a famous comedienne, this hit show of the 1964 season contained such songs as "People" and "Don't Rain on My Parade." For a two-parter: name (a) the show, (b) the main character, and (c) the star.

54 A long-running hit musical, which opened in 1965, featured a loony old man, his sidekick, and his "quest." Name the show and the character on which it is based.

55 An extraordinarily popular musical comedy of 1949 has a daring treatment of racial prejudice, concerned with a plantation owner's children by a former marriage as well as with a romance between a young naval officer and a Polynesian beauty. One of the songs suggests that "They Have to Be Carefully Taught" to be prejudiced against other races. Can you name the show?

56 When this musical play opened in 1904, it marked several "firsts" for a brash young composer who had no formal musical training, was born of vaudeville parents, and had worked the vaudeville circuit himself. It was his first show in a major Broadway theater, the first show with his long-time partner, Sam Harris, and his first solid hit. The show features a flag-waving American jockey who goes to England to ride in races there. Who was the composer, and what is the name of this show?

57 This team of composers was unique in that they also collaborated on the lyrics to their musical comedy songs. Their two biggest hits were unusual comic shows, one about labor-management difficulties at a factory, and one about a perennially losing baseball team that received supernatural assistance. Can you name the composers and their shows?

58 This composer, who fled from Russia at the time of the Revolution there, happened to see the sheet music of George Gershwin's "Swanee." This gave him the inspiration to write popular music, and he became famous for a musical starring Ethel Waters and another starring Eddie Cantor. Name the composer and these two shows.

59 One writing team has had the longest collaboration in the history of the

Broadway musical theater. They wrote lyrics for many shows, including *On the Town* (1944), *Peter Pan* (1950), *Two on the Aisle* (1951), *Wonderful Town* (1953), and *Bells Are Ringing* (1956). Name these two clever lyricists.

60 What is the famous folk opera, set in Charleston, South Carolina, that has been presented by the Metropolitan Opera Company and opera houses all over Europe, as well as on Broadway?

61 This hit musical comedy was based on a comic strip about some grotesque characters in the mythical town of Dogpatch. It features a comedy song, "Jubilation T. Cornpone." The lyricist is better known than the composer. Can you name them and their successful show?

62 A wonderful hit musical comedy, which features marching band music and a realistic picture of life in a small American town in 1912, had book, lyrics, and music by one person. He also wrote a show about a wealthy Colorado eccentric who survived the sinking of the *Titanic*. Can you name the versatile composer and his two shows?

63 Called a "rock opera," this Andrew Lloyd Webber musical, which opened in 1971, shocked and offended many religious denominations, but had a successful run. One of its songs was "I Don't Know How to Love Him." Name the show.

64 Webber also scored solid hits in London and New York with a musical about a South American political figure (1976) and with a spectacularly staged show, partly set in the Paris sewers (1986). Name the shows.

65 This musical, which opened in London in 1961, had a circus setting, a character named Littlechap, and a variety of hit songs, including "What Kind of Fool Am I?" For a two-parter, can you name: (a) the show, and (b) the composer and lyricist?

66 Although this 1933 Jerome Kern musical was not particularly well received, it had a longer-than-average run due largely to the success of one song that has become a classic, "Smoke Gets In Your Eyes." Can you name the musical?

67 Set in Scandinavia and Rome in 1860, this 1944 operetta was adapted from music by Edvard Grieg and featured the Ballet Russe de Monte Carlo in one of its numbers. Can you name it?

68 Comedy stars Bert Williams, W.C. Fields, Fanny Brice, Leon Errol, Will Rogers and Eddie Cantor had one thing in common. They all appeared in shows developed by the most celebrated producer in Broadway history. Name him.

69 Although the theatrical genius in the preceding question was best known for the series of Broadway reviews that bore his name, he also produced a number of musical comedies by various composers and lyricists. Can you name three of his landmark shows?

70 To take advantage of the talents of black performers, a musical comedy called *The Wiz* opened on Broadway in 1975, with music and lyrics by Charlie Smalls. On what children's classic was this show based?

Answers

① *Noel Coward (1899–1973). He also wrote the popular waltz song, "I'll Follow My Secret Heart" as well as the witty songs "Mad Dogs and Englishmen" and "The Stately Homes of England."*

② *John Philip Sousa (1854–1932), who wrote* El Capitan *(1896). The most famous music in the operetta is the rousing title march.*

③ H.M.S. Pinafore *(1878), so popular that 10,000 copies of the musical score were sold in one day.*

④ *The choices are many:* Thespis, Trial by Jury, Yeomen of the Guard, The Sorcerer, The Pirates of Penzance, Patience, Iolanthe, The Peer and the Peri, Princess Ida, The Mikado, The Gondoliers, *and* Ruddigore.

⑤ *Victor Herbert (1859–1924). Born in Dublin, he was trained as a cellist.*

⑥ *Herbert's operettas included* Babette *(1903),* Mlle. Modiste *(1905),* The Red Mill *(1906),* Naughty Marietta *(1910),* Sweethearts *(1913), and* Eileen *(1917).*

⑦ *(a) Irving Berlin (1888–1989), (b)* This Is the Army *(1942),* Annie Get Your Gun *(1946), and* Call Me Madam *(1950).*

⑧ The Vagabond King, *which premiered in 1925, starring Dennis King, a Shakespearean actor and excellent singer.*

⑨ *(a)* Show Boat, *by (b) Jerome Kern (1885–1945).*

⑩ *Sigmund Romberg (1887–1951), who wrote* The New Moon, *which contains songs with less ambiguous titles such as "One Kiss" and "Stout-Hearted Men."*

⑪ *This popular operetta is* The Student Prince *(1924).*

⑫ Maytime *(1917) and* Blossom Time *(1921).*

⑬ *Johann Strauss (1825–99), composer of* Die Fledermaus *(1873) and* Zigeunerbaron (The Gypsy Baron) *(1874).*

⑭ *Franz Lehár (1870–1947), who wrote* Die lustige Witwe (The Merry Widow).

⑮ *Kurt Weill (1900–50). The works were* The Three-Penny Opera, *1933 (Brecht);* Lady in the Dark, *1941 (Hart); and* One Touch of Venus, *1943 (Nash).*

⑯ Sweeney Todd *(1979) and* Into the Woods *(1987).*

⑰ *Choose from* A Funny Thing Happened on the Way to the Forum *(1962)*, Anyone Can Whistle *(1964)*, Company *(1970)*, Follies *(1971)*, A Little Night Music *(1973)*, Pacific Overtures *(1976)*, Merrily We Roll Along *(1981)*, Sunday In the Park With George *(1984)*.

⑱ West Side Story *(1957)*.

⑲ *(a)* Richard Rodgers *(1902–79) and Lorenz Hart (1895–1943), (b) Rodgers, and (c)* The Girl Friend *(1926)*, A Connecticut Yankee *(1927)*, Jumbo *(1935)*, On Your Toes *(1936)*, Babes in Arms *(1937)*, I'd Rather Be Right *(1937), and* Pal Joey *(1940)*.

⑳ *The show, based on Damon Runyon stories, is* Guys and Dolls *(1950)*, *written by Frank Loesser (1910–69)*.

㉑ Leonard Bernstein *(1918–90), who wrote the score for* Candide. *The librettists were the playwright Lillian Hellman and the poet Richard Wilbur.*

㉒ *The word is* pasticcio, *which can also mean a jumble or mess.*

㉓ *The show was* Jumbo *(1935) by Richard Rodgers and Lorenz Hart.*

㉔ *(a)* Richard Rodgers *(1902–79) and Oscar Hammerstein (1895–1960), (b)* Oklahoma. *The greatest financial success Broadway had seen in many years, it earned its backers millions of dollars.*

㉕ The Sound of Music.

㉖ A Funny Thing Happened on the Way to the Forum *(1962), by Stephen Sondheim.*

㉗ *1(d), 2(c), 3(e), 4(b), 5(a).*

㉘ *1(b), 2(e), 3(d), 4(a), 5(c).*

㉙ *1(d), 2(e), 3(a), 4(c), 5(b). All of these operettas are by Victor Herbert.*

㉚ *1(c), 2(a), 3(j), 4(e), 5(f), 6(b), 7(i), 8(h), 9(g), 10(d).*

㉛ *(a) Rudolf Friml (1879–1972); (b)* Rose-Marie *(1924), which was King George V's favorite. It was very popular as a 1936 movie starring Jeanette MacDonald and Nelson Eddy, with its featured song, "Indian Love Call."*

㉜ *It was* Of Thee I Sing *(1931), with music by George Gershwin (1898–1937) and lyrics by Ira Gershwin (1896–1983).*

㉝ My Fair Lady *(1956), by Alan Jay Lerner (1918–86), who wrote the lyrics, and Frederick Loewe (1901–88), who wrote the music.*

㉞ Brigadoon *(1947).*

㉟ Camelot *(1960).*

㊱ *An Englishman,* John Gay *(1685–1732), who wrote* The Beggar's Opera.

㊲ The Mikado *(1885). It has continued to be popular, and in 1978 it was produced in London with an all-black cast and entitled* The Black Mikado.

㊳ Paint Your Wagon, *which opened in New York in 1951. It was written by Lerner and Loewe.*

㊴ *Cole Porter (1891– 1964) wrote the music and lyrics for* Kiss Me, Kate.

㊵ A Little Night Music *(1973), which features the poignant song "Send in the Clowns."*

㊶ On Your Toes *(1936) by Richard Rodgers and Lorenz Hart.*

㊷ Miss Saigon, *by Alain Boubil and Claude-Michel Schönberg. The show, which was already a roaring success in London, has a helicopter descend on the stage and take refugees roaring away.*

㊸ *Composer John Kander and lyricist Fred Ebb wrote the musical* Cabaret, *starring Joel Grey.*

㊹ *It was Jerry Herman (1932–   ), who wrote the brilliant music and lyrics for* La Cage Aux Folles.

㊺ *Other shows by Herman include* Milk and Honey *(1961)*, Hello Dolly *(1964), and* Mame *(1966).*

(46) *Cole Porter wrote the music and lyrics for* Anything Goes.

(47) Cats *(1981), by Andrew Lloyd Webber (1948–   ).*

(48) Les Misérables *was produced by the team of Claude-Michel Schönberg, composer; Alain Boublil, conception and original text; and Herbert Kretzmer, lyricist.*

(49) *The producer Michael Bennett (1943–1987) is given the principal credit for* A Chorus Line, *but Marvin Hamlisch (1944–   ) wrote the excellent music.*

(50) *The composer is Roger Miller (1936–   ), who is known for such songs as "Dang Me," "King of the Road," and "Chug-A-Lug." He received the 1985 Tony Award for the music and lyrics to the show* Big River.

(51) *(a)* Fiddler on the Roof, *(b) composer: Jerry Bock (1928–   ), lyricist: Sheldon Harnick (1924–   ), (c) Teyve.*

(52) The Fantasticks, *with music by Harvey Schmidt (1929–   ) and lyrics and book by Tom Jones (1928–   ). It is based on Edmond Rostand's play* Les Romanesques *and concerns two fathers who try to make their children fall in love by pretending to disapprove.*

(53) *(a)* Funny Girl, *music by Jule Styne (1905–   ), lyrics by Bob Merrill (1921–   ), (b) Fanny Brice, (c) Barbra Streisand.*

(54) Man of La Mancha, *with music by Mitch Leigh (1928–) and lyrics by Joe Darion (1917–), based on Cervantes' character Don Quixote. One of its beautiful songs is "The Impossible Dream."*

(55) South Pacific, *by Rodgers and Hammerstein.*

(56) *George M. Cohan (1878–1942), who continued with many Broadway successes, nearly all with unabashedly patriotic tunes. The show was* Little Johnny Jones. *It features the famous songs, "The Yankee Doodle Boy," and "Give My Regards to Broadway."*

(57) *The popular team was Richard Adler (1923–) and Jerry Ross (1926–55), who wrote* Pajama Game *and* Damn Yankees.

(58) *Vernon Duke (1903–69), who wrote* Cabin in the Sky *(1940), starring Ethel Waters, and* Banjo Eyes *(1941), with Eddie Cantor.*

(59) *Betty Comden (1919–) and Adolph Green (1915–).*

(60) Porgy and Bess *by George Gershwin, first presented in 1935.*

(61) *Gene DePaul (1919–) wrote the music and Johnny Mercer (1909–76) the lyrics. The show was* L'il Abner *(1956).*

⑥② *Meredith Willson (1902–84) is the composer and lyricist of* The Music Man *(1957) and* The Unsinkable Molly Brown *(1960).*

⑥③ Jesus Christ Superstar.

⑥④ Evita, *about South American Evita Peron, and* The Phantom of the Opera.

⑥⑤ *(a)* Stop the World—I Want to Get Off, *(b) Leslie Bricusse (1931–) and Anthony Newley (1931–).*

⑥⑥ Roberta. *Entertainer Bob Hope got his start in this show.*

⑥⑦ Song of Norway.

⑥⑧ *Flamboyant showman Florenz Ziegfeld (1867–1932).*

⑥⑨ *The best-known shows produced by Ziegfeld are* Sally *(1920),* Rio Rita *and* Show Boat *(1927),* The Three Musketeers *and* Whoopee *(1928), and* Bittersweet *(1929).*

⑦⓪ The Wonderful Wizard of Oz, *by L. Frank Baum. The motion picture* The Wizard of Oz *(1938) starred Judy Garland and featured a song by Harold Arlen (1905–86) and E.Y. (Yip) Harburg (1898–1981) called "Over the Rainbow."*

Jazz: America's Great Contribution

O*ne of America's most important contributions to music is jazz, which was born in New Orleans of African-American roots and has since gained worldwide popularity and influenced such major composers as Debussy, Gershwin, and Stravinsky. This highly rhythmic and original music, played by musicians who freely invent variations on themes as they perform, is not to be confused with rock music or the Tin Pan Alley popular ballads, though these types of music were influenced by jazz and are often included in a loose definition of the term. How familiar are you with America's chief musical export? Let's find out.*

❶ Some of the earliest jazz in New Orleans was heard from brass bands at funerals, playing a slow, mournful blues on the way to the cemetery and a lively jazz tune on the return. One upbeat tune predominates for the latter use. What is the title?

② Louis Armstrong, an all-time great jazz musician, once gave a classic reply to a reporter who asked him "What is jazz?" Can you quote or paraphrase his answer?

③ Jazz musicians use a tune as a base, but add their personal interpretations and change the melody as they perform "solos." What is the musical term for this creative practice?

④ One important element in the formation of jazz was ragtime, highly syncopated music with a heavily accented beat, popular from about 1895 to 1920. A pianist and composer was the first famous exponent of ragtime, and his compositions, such as "Maple Leaf Rag," are still being played. Name him.

⑤ The origin of the word *jazz* is uncertain. Some theorize that it comes from a French word, used commonly in New Orleans, *jaser*, which means literally "to chatter," but has sexual overtones in its slang usage. Others say it derives from "chas" (from the name Charles), honoring the name of the first great New Orleans jazz man (who was known by the nickname "Buddy"). Can you name this cornet player?

6 The most written-about jazz musician of all time began playing piano in New Orleans bordellos in 1902, the year when, he claimed, he "invented jazz." Also a composer, he wrote many jazz classics, including "King Porter Stomp," "Wolverine Blues," and "Wild Man Blues." Name him.

7 This famous cornet player from Davenport, Iowa, crossed racial lines to learn jazz from such great musicians as Jimmy Noone. His recordings with the Wolverines and with Paul Whiteman's orchestra brought him prominence after his death at age twenty-eight. Who was he?

8 The first great jazz trumpeter took his New Orleans music to Chicago, where he formed the Creole Jazz Band, the first band of black musicians to make a series of recordings. Name him.

9 One of the young stars of the Creole Jazz Band was Louis Armstrong, who accidentally developed a new style of singing when he forgot the lyrics of a song during a recording session and used nonsense syllables instead of words. What is the name given to this style of singing, later used by Cab Calloway and Ella Fitzgerald?

10 Although many consider him the best trumpeter in jazz history, Armstrong made one of his best-selling records in 1964 with a pop tune, singing and playing the title song from a Broadway musical. Name the song.

⓫ Jazz by white musicians became popular in 1917, when a band opened at Reisenweber's Club in New York and their recordings became a national craze. Though they were clearly imitating African-American styles, they called themselves the "creators of jazz." Name the leader and the band.

⓬ On February 24, 1924, at the Aeolian Hall in New York, a symphonic work using jazz rhythms and forms was given its premiere performance by Paul Whiteman's Orchestra. For a two-parter, (a) name the composer, and (b) the famous innovative piece of music.

⓭ Some jazz musicians have colorful "monikers." Try matching the following nicknames on the left with the famous last names on the right.

Nickname	Last Name
1. Bird	(a) Adderley
2. Cannonball	(b) Gillespie
3. Satchmo	(c) Waller
4. Dizzy	(d) Parker
5. Fats	(e) Armstrong

⓮ Besides King Oliver, another jazz musician had the royal nickname "King." He was a pianist who achieved his greatest fame singing ballads such as "Nature Boy." Name him.

⓯ Speaking of royal nick-names, can you identify two jazz band leaders with royal titles below the rank of king?

⓰ An American novelist gave the name "Jazz Age" to the decade of the 1920s because he believed that jazz was identified with the era's characteristics of excess, exuberance, sin, and license. Name the novelist.

⓱ In the 1930s jazz music moved to large dance halls and ballrooms, and big bands began to play it. The word *jazz* was commonly replaced by another word. What was it?

⓲ New York City in the 1930s had a number of ballrooms in hotels, and they became widely known from the dance music broadcast over the radio. Match these ballrooms with the hotels.

Ballroom	Hotel
1. Blue Room	**(a)** Lexington
2. Palm Room	**(b)** Biltmore
3. Terrace Room	**(c)** Commodore
4. Moonlit Terrace	**(d)** New Yorker
5. Green Room	**(e)** Edison
6. Manhattan Room	**(f)** Lincoln
7. Grill Room	**(g)** Pennsylvania

⓳ A three-hour radio program every Saturday night over NBC Radio began in 1935 and presented one of America's best big bands to a jazz-crazed America. Name the show and the band leader.

❷⓿ The bandleader in the preceding question was innovative in presenting jazz in small combinations of musicians, called "combos." First was his trio, with the leader playing clarinet. Can you name the drummer and the pianist? For extra credit, can you name the jazz man who turned the trio into a quartet?

❷❶ Can you match the leaders of the big bands on the left with their theme songs on the right?

Band	**Theme Song**
1. Tommy Dorsey	**(a)** "Take the A Train"
2. Glen Gray	**(b)** "Begin the Beguine"
3. Cab Calloway	**(c)** "Flyin' Home"
4. Glenn Miller	**(d)** "I'm Getting Sentimental Over You."
5. Duke Ellington	**(e)** "One O'Clock Jump"
6. Lionel Hampton	**(f)** "Smoke Rings"
7. Artie Shaw	**(g)** "Moonlight Serenade"
8. Larry Clinton	**(h)** "Woodchopper's Ball"
9. Count Basie	**(i)** "Minnie the Moocher"
10. Woody Herman	**(j)** "The Dipsy Doodle"

❷❷ Do you know which solo instruments the big bandleaders played? Try matching them.

Leader	Instrument
1. Tommy Dorsey	**(a)** trumpet
2. Duke Ellington	**(b)** trombone
3. Louis Prima	**(c)** piano
4. Glenn Miller	**(d)** drums
5. Gene Krupa	**(e)** saxophone
6. Artie Shaw	**(f)** clarinet
7. Jimmy Dorsey	**(g)** violin
8. Erskine Hawkins	**(h)** vibraphone
9. Harry James	
10. Joe Venuti	
11. Lionel Hampton	
12. Woody Herman	
13. Bunny Berigan	
14. Jack Teagarden	
15. Ray McKinley	

❷❸ The big band era was enlivened by some outstanding vocalists who were forever linked with certain orchestras. Can you match these bands with their singers?

Band	Singer
1. Stan Kenton	**(a)** Jo Stafford
2. Les Brown	**(b)** Peggy Lee
3. Chick Webb	**(c)** June Christy
4. Woody Herman	**(d)** Doris Day

Band	**Singer**
5. Benny Goodman	**(e)** Marion Hutton
6. Tommy Dorsey	**(f)** Ella Fitzgerald
7. Glenn Miller	**(g)** Helen O'Connell
8. Jimmy Dorsey	**(h)** Frances Wayne
9. Paul Whiteman	**(i)** Bea Wain
10. Larry Clinton	**(j)** Mildred Bailey

24 One of the greatest American singers left a big jazz band in the 1940s to go on his own. He made music history when he opened at the Paramount Theater in New York on Columbus Day, 1944. For days, traffic in the Times Square area was disrupted for pedestrians and automobiles as thousands of teen-agers, mostly young women, milled about and lined up for tickets. Inside the theater, they swooned and screamed as he sang. Who was he?

25 Just after World War II, a new kind of jazz appeared, promoted by the trumpet player Dizzy Gillespie and his combo. The name came from nonsense syllables Dizzy often sang. What was the music called?

26 The only jazz artist to become famous playing the soprano saxophone was not fully recognized until he went to France, where he became a national star of the Maurice Chevalier class. Name him.

27 The great jazz bands of the thirties and forties featured "sidemen," who played their instruments in ensembles and also in improvised solo passages. Some of them were almost as famous as the band leaders. Match these bands with their sidemen.

Band	**Sideman**
1. Duke Ellington	**(a)** Lester Young, sax
2. Benny Goodman	**(b)** Ray McKinley, drums
3. Count Basie	**(c)** Barney Bigard, clarinet
4. Bob Crosby	**(d)** James Young, trombone
5. Jimmy Dorsey	**(e)** Flip Phillips, sax
6. Tommy Dorsey	**(f)** Ziggy Elman, trumpet
7. Jimmy Lunceford	**(g)** George Auld, sax
8. Woody Herman	**(h)** Bob Haggart, bass
9. Stan Kenton	**(i)** Vido Musso, sax
10. Artie Shaw	**(j)** Charlie Spivak, trumpet

28 Another unusual jazz instrument is the baritone saxophone. The leading jazz man on this instrument was the first to organize a jazz quartet without a piano. He also was an arranger for Stan Kenton. Who was he?

29 What string bass player made a smash hit with a number called "Big Noise from Winnetka," played as a duet with drummer Ray Bauduc?

30 He was the first modern jazz musician to play single-string solos on an electric guitar, starring with the Benny Goodman Orchestra. Name him.

31 One of the most famous of all blues singers was the subject of a 1984 Broadway play by August Wilson. One of her best-known recordings is "Black Bottom," named for a dance then in vogue. Name her.

32 The singer in the previous question had a protégée who became even more famous, earning the title "Empress of Blues" for such outstanding recordings (accompanied by such artists as Louis Armstrong and Fletcher Henderson) as "Gimme a Pigfoot" and "Nobody Knows You When You're Down and Out." Who was she?

33 Topping most of the jazz polls in the 1950s and 1960s was a classically trained pianist who led his quartet (also featuring Paul Desmond on alto-sax) on best-selling albums such as *Gone With the Wind* and *Jazz Goes to College*. Name him.

34 What popular American jazz artist also played classical music and commissioned Bela Bartok, Aaron Copeland, and Paul Hindemith to write clarinet concertos for him?

35 "Sophisticated Lady" and "Mood Indigo" were popular numbers for this band, but its pianist leader also composed an extended composition, *Black, Brown, and Beige*, which ran about fifty minutes in its original form, played at Carnegie Hall in January 1943. Name the composer and band leader.

36 Beginning in the 1930s and continuing into the later 1970s this band was one of the most powerful and swinging of all the big bands. It featured one of the great rhythm sections: the leader on piano; Jo Jones, drums; Walter Page, bass; and Freddie Green, guitar. Who led the band?

37 Although too old to be drafted, this popular swing band leader volunteered for the Army Air Corps in World War II and assembled an outstanding armed forces orchestra made up of musicians from some of the era's best bands. On December 15, 1944, he flew from England across the Channel in a small plane, to make arrangements for his band's arrival in Paris, and presumably died in a plane crash at sea. Name him.

38 This great jazz singer, who has long been ranked at the top by jazz buffs, made three memorable albums with Louis Armstrong (including *Porgy and Bess*). In April, 1958, she gave a Carnegie Hall concert with Duke Ellington to celebrate her *Duke Ellington Songbook* album. Name her.

❸❾ From 1933–35 this saxophone player led a band that included his trombonist brother, another trombonist named Glenn Miller, drummer Ray McKinley, and singer Bob Crosby, brother of Bing. All five later led well-known bands. Who was the leader and his brother?

❹❶ In the 1940s bands led by Bob Crosby and Muggsy Spanier revived interest in a type of jazz that had begun in New Orleans and was later given a somewhat new style in Chicago. The name given this form of jazz in the forties is the name still used today. What is it?

Answers

① Probably the best-known Dixieland Song, "When the Saints Go Marching In."

② "If you have to ask, you'll never understand it."

③ Improvisation, which is an important element in true jazz. Improvisation has been defined as "composing on the spur of the moment," or "composing and performing simultaneously."

④ Scott Joplin (1868–1917). His ragtime tune, "The Entertainer," was featured in the 1973 Oscar-winning best picture, The Sting, *with Paul Newman and Robert Redford.*

⑤ *The legendary Charles "Buddy" Bolden (1868–1931).*

⑥ *Innovative pianist Jelly Roll Morton (1885–1941).*

⑦ *The legendary Bix Beiderbecke (1903–31).*

⑧ *Joseph (King) Oliver (1885–1938). Louis Armstrong makes it clear in his autobiography,* Satchmo, *that Oliver was his true idol and only real musical mentor.*

⑨ *"Scat" singing.*

⑩ *"Hello, Dolly."*

⑪ *Nick LaRocca (1889–1962), cornetist and leader of the "Original Dixieland Jazz Band."*

⑫ *(a) George Gershwin (1898–1937), (b)* Rhapsody in Blue.

⑬ *1(d), 2(a), 3(e), 4(b), 5(c).*

⑭ *Jazz pianist and pop singer Nat "King" Cole (1919–68).*

⑮ *Count Basie (1904–84), whose band was the first from the U.S.A. to play a command performance for the Queen of England, and Duke Ellington (1899–1974).*

⑯ *F. Scott Fitzgerald (1896–1940), author of* The Great Gatsby, Tender Is the Night, *and* The Far Side of Paradise.

⑰ *"Swing." There were two kinds of swing: hot (more jazz oriented, used for a fast dance called "the jitterbug") and sweet (slower, smoother music for dancing).*

⑱ *1(f), 2(c), 3(d), 4(b), 5(e), 6(g), 7(a).*

⑲ "Let's Dance," Benny Goodman (1909–86).

⑳ Gene Krupa, drums, and Teddy Wilson, piano. Lionel Hampton, playing vibraphone, as well as occasionally drums and piano, made the threesome a quartet.

㉑ 1(d), 2(f), 3(i), 4(g), 5(a), 6(c), 7(b), 8(j), 9(e), 10(h).

㉒ 1(b), 2(c), 3(a), 4(b), 5(d), 6(f), 7(e), 8(a), 9(a), 10(g), 11(h), 12(f), 13(a), 14(b), 15(d).

㉓ 1(c), 2(d), 3(f), 4(h), 5(b), 6(a), 7(e), 8(g), 9(j), 10(i).

㉔ "Old Blue Eyes," Frank Sinatra (1915–   ), still a superstar in the 1990s.

㉕ "Bop," "Rebop," or "Bebop." This music is characterized by a whirlwind velocity, with frequent duet passages, played in close harmony by the trumpet and saxophone.

㉖ The expatriate was Sidney Bechet (1897–1959).

㉗ 1(c), 2(f), 3(a), 4(h), 5(b), 6(j), 7(d), 8(e), 9(i), 10(j).

㉘ Influential jazzman, Gerry Mulligan (1927–   ).

㉙ Bob Haggart. He recorded the number with the Bob Crosby Orchestra.

㉚ This expert guitarist was Charles Christian (1919–42).

㉛ Gertrude "Ma" Rainey (1886–1939).

㉜ Bessie Smith (1894–1937). In 1970 Columbia Records launched a giant project to reissue almost everything she had recorded, resulting in five double-album sets.

㉝ Dave Brubeck (1920–), who studied composition under Arnold Schoenberg and Darius Milhaud. In December, 1959, his quartet appeared with Leonard Bernstein and the New York Philharmonic, performing Dialogue for Jazz Combo and Symphony, composed by his brother, Howard Brubeck.

㉞ Clarinetist Benny Goodman (1909–86), a child prodigy who joined the musician's union at age thirteen.

㉟ Edward Kennedy (Duke) Ellington (1899–1974).

㊱ The legendary William (Count) Basie (1904–84).

㊲ Glenn Miller (1904–44), whose band was renowned for such numbers as "In the Mood," "Little Brown Jug," and "Chattanooga Choo Choo."

㊳ *Ella Fitzgerald (1918–).*
Fellow musicians praise her for a "bell-like clarity of tone, flexibility of range, and rhythmic brilliance of style."

㊴ *Jimmy Dorsey (1904–57) and Tommy Dorsey (1905–56). They were sons of a music teacher in Shenandoah, Pennsylvania.*

㊵ *Dixieland jazz. Spanier (1906–67) revived and rearranged such early favorites as "Dipper Mouth Blues" and "I Wish I Could Shimmy Like My Sister Kate." Bob Crosby (1913–) had constant requests for "South Rampart Street Parade" and "Muskrat Ramble."*

Instrumental and Chamber Music

Some of the most exciting music is played in solo by brilliant instrumentalists: masters of the piano like Vladimir Horowitz, violinists like Itzhak Perlman, trumpeters like Maurice André or cellists like Gregor Piatigorsky. Also, some of the most interesting musical lore concerns these and other famous musicians.

Less in the spotlight, but no less important musically, is chamber music, written to be played in smaller rooms than concert halls. Such music embraces works for small combinations of instruments: sonatas for solo instruments and piano; trios; quartets; quintets; sextets; septets; octets. Some of the world's greatest composers—Bach, Beethoven, Moz-

art, Schubert—have been at their most creative writing chamber music.

Let's begin with a violinist whose performances were so sensational that they inspired legends.

1 One of the greatest violinists of all time made his debut at age thirteen in Genoa. From age nineteen to twenty-three he temporarily retired for further study, and when he returned to the concert stage in 1805, he was a sensation. In 1809 Franz Lehar wrote an operetta about him. Name him.

2 The violinist in the preceding question was also the composer of a virtuoso violin piece that moves at an almost impossibly fast tempo. It is often played as an encore by concert violinists. Give the title.

3 Much admired as a composer for his piano music, particularly the exciting Hungarian Rhapsodies, he became a flamboyant showman when he gave concerts, using cheap theatrical tricks and inferior music to advertise his phenomenal piano technique. Who was this musician?

4 A great composer had a particular love for the clavichord. For this instrument he wrote a collection of forty-eight preludes and fugues. What was the collection called?

5 One of the great piano virtuosos of his day, this Russian composer wrote some of the finest works for this instrument. His melodic *Prelude in C-Sharp Minor* is still popular and is frequently performed. Who was he?

6 The slow movement of this string quartet is one of the most famous pieces in Russian chamber music. The melody became popular in the U.S. when it was used in the hit song, "And This Is My Beloved," from the musical comedy *Kismet* (1953) by Robert Wright and George Forrest. Who was the Russian composer?

7 This English composer was the first musician to be buried in Westminster Abbey, where he had been the principal organist. He found the harpsichord an attractive medium for composition and greatly increased the technical possibilities of that instrument. Who was he?

8 In 1954 a distinguished harpsichordist completed the recording of Bach's *The Well-Tempered Clavier.* It had taken her over a half century of scholarly research to recreate the musical notations as Bach intended them. Who was this musician, who called these recordings her "last will and testament" to the world?

9 After his debut in Berlin, this eleven-year-old Russian violinist played at a party for some of the world's most famous violinists. When he finished, the great Fritz Kreisler stood up, looked at the other celebrated musicians, and said, "Well, gentleman, we can now all break our violins across our knees." Name the young virtuoso.

10 This greatest of all Polish composers (and most Polish of all great composers) was presented with a silver urn containing some Polish earth when he left his native land. He never forgot the land of his birth, and this urn was buried with him in Paris. He wrote eleven piano works in the Polonaise form. Name him.

11 When his *String Quartet No. 1* was introduced in 1907, the unfamiliar sound led to a riot in the concert hall. Subsequent performances brought laughter, hisses, and even fist fights. Name this composer who helped develop the innovative twelve-tone system and had a profound influence on modern music.

12 One of the greatest musical prodigies of all time began producing melodies and pleasing chords at the harpsichord when he was only three years old. By the time he was six he had written several charming pieces for the harpsichord and part of a concerto. Name him.

13 A set of three string quartets from his middle period are among the finest that Beethoven composed. They were commissioned by a Russian count who was an ambassador to Austria, and they bear his name. By what name does the music world know them?

14 This Italian composer wrote about 180 piano pieces that were gathered under the general title of *Sins of My Old Age*. These compositions have unusual titles, including *Four Hors d'oeuvres, or Radishes, Anchovies, Gherkin and Butter Themes in Variation*. Another is called *Castor Oil*. Who is this imaginative composer?

15 One of the world's most beloved pieces of chamber music is the *Quintet in A Major*, known as *Die Forelle*, or *Trout*. It incorporates the lilting German song, *Die Forelle*, in an original work that uses a piano, violin, viola, cello, and double bass. Who composed it?

16 What is the musical term, meaning literally a "trifle," for a short instrumental composition, and what composer is associated with it?

17 Give the term for the musical exercise in which a particular technical problem is posed for the instrumentalist to practice.

18 This French composer, who influenced Debussy, wrote many piano pieces and gave them whimsical names such as

"Flabby Preludes for a Dog," and "Dessicated Embryos." His instructions on the playing of his works included "to be played dry as a cuckoo, light as an egg" and "like a nightingale with a toothache." Who was he?

19 What prolific composer of piano music fell in love with, and eventually married, his teacher's daughter, Clara, who became the greatest woman pianist of her generation?

20 A story is told that during a thunderstorm, this composer entered a blacksmith's shop in order to stay dry. He heard the steady beat of the blacksmith's hammer and was inspired to write a piece for the harpsichord (now most often played on the piano). Give the composer and the title of this work.

21 What composer was a master of brief compositions for the piano in the form of the *Moment Musicale*?

22 One of this composer's frequently played piano compositions is a series of eleven piano pieces suggesting the beauties of a certain insect. Name the composer and the piano work.

23 Although his piano sonatas may be better music, piano students love this short piano piece. It is dedicated, in the title, to a young lady who was never identified. Name the composer and the piece.

24 One of the world's most popular melodies is found in the *Andante Cantabile* movement of this Russian composer's first string quartet. The story goes that, as he was about to begin the slow movement of this quartet, the composer heard a plasterer humming this plaintive folk melody while working. Name the composer.

25 Which French composer, most of whose music was written for the solo piano, is considered the chief representative of impressionism?

26 Writing music for children that is also a delight for adult audiences was a special talent for the composer of *Kinderscenen (Scenes from Childhood)*. The most celebrated of these pieces is "Träumerei." Who composed it?

27 In the mid-1930s, he became the first pianistic hero of the electrical era of recording by producing the first complete recorded Chopin series in history. His highly charged, disciplined, yet emotional playing won him many fans. Can you name him?

28 Everyone knows about the great violins made by Antonio Stradivari (1644–1737) and his sons. Many of the famous Stradivarius violins have names such as "La Pucelle" or "the Alard" (considered the finest of all). But who was the Italian violin maker who produced instruments considered nearly equal to those by Stradivari?

㉙ This composer, who has been called the "father of French piano music," wrote four volumes of music, collectively entitled *Pièces de clavecin*. Many of the pieces are programmatic, descriptive of bees, gnats, butterflies, reapers, grape-gatherers, jugglers, and the gossip of court life. Who was this composer?

㉚ Let's try a Matching Question. Match the well-known works for the piano on the left with their composers on the right.

Work	Composer
1. *Clair de lune*	(a) Grieg
2. *Blumenstück*	(b) Beethoven
3. *Goldberg Variations*	(c) Chopin
4. *Norwegian Peasant March*	(d) Schubert
5. *Pathetique Sonata*	(e) Debussy
6. *Military Polonaise*	(f) Liszt
7. *Variations on a Theme by Handel*	(g) Bach
8. *Impromptu in B Flat*	(h) Brahms
9. *Songs Without Words*	(i) Schumann
10. *Vallée d'Obermann*	(j) Mendelssohn

31 Now match the famous violin pieces on the left with their composers.

Work	Composer
1. *Träumerei*	(a) Schubert
2. *Carnaval de Venise*	(b) Brahms
3. *Hungarian Dances*	(c) Kreisler
4. *Capriccio Brilliant*	(d) Ravel
5. *Spanish Dance (Habañera)*	(e) Schumann
6. *Kreutzer Sonata*	(f) Mendelssohn
7. *Ave Maria*	(g) Sarasate
8. *Tzigane*	(h) Beethoven
9. *Mephisto Waltz*	(i) Liszt
10. *Caprice Viennois*	(j) Paganini

32 In 1915 an American composer wrote a piano sonata called *Concord* which was many years ahead of its time. It has bold experiments in harmonics and tonalities. Who was the composer?

33 An innovative composer of this century amazed his peers by writing music for a "prepared piano." This altered type of piano has dampers of metal, wood, rubber, felt, and other materials stuffed between the strings in carefully measured positions in order to produce new tone qualities. Name him.

34 During his great career this violinist played many pieces which he said were transcriptions of the works by obscure old masters. When New York music critic Olin Downes tried to trace the source of his arrangement of Pugnani's *Praeludium and Allegro*, he learned that this piece and many others were original with the violinist. Who was this modest composer?

㉟ After his family became poverty-stricken following the Russian Revolution, this legendary pianist left Russia for good. After an illustrious career in America and Europe, he returned to his homeland for the first time in 1988, where he gave outstanding performances at the age of eighty-four. Name him.

㊱ Although his colleagues did not consider him to be a great technician or a great musician, this Polish-born pianist was the most popular and highest paid musician of his day. At a 1902 Carnegie Hall concert he was mobbed by hysterical women, causing him to lose a watch given to him by the czar. Name this pianist.

㊲ The only African-American to achieve superstar status as a classical pianist was born in Nuremberg, Germany, where his father was a soldier in the U.S. army. One critic wrote: "More than any other pianist, his performances are reminiscent of what a Liszt concert must have been like." Name him.

Answers

① *Niccolò Paganini (1782–1840). He introduced a number of completely new violin techniques, including the left-hand and right-hand pizzicato (or plucking the strings), ricochet bowing, and solos on a single string. His playing was so brilliant that he was accused of gaining his unusual technique in an unearthly and supernatural way.*

② *The title of the piece is* Moto perpetuo *("Perpetual Motion").*

③ *Franz Liszt (1811–86). He was the originator of the piano recital and the first to give an entire concert without an orchestra or assisting musicians.*

④ The Well-Tempered Clavier, *or* The Well-Tempered Clavichord *by Johann Sebastian Bach (1685–1750).*

⑤ *Serge Rachmaninoff (1873–1943). Ironically, he made little money from the composition, despite its fabulous sales, because he neglected to copyright it.*

⑥ *Alexander Borodin (1833–87). He wrote this famous third movement (a "Nocturne") of his String Quartet in D Major.*

⑦ *Henry Purcell (1659–95), the greatest composer produced by England up to his day; some critics call him the greatest English composer.*

⑧ *The famous harpsichordist Wanda Landowska (1877–1959).*

⑨ *The amazing prodigy was Jascha Heifetz (1901–87).*

⑩ *The patriotic Frederic Chopin (1810–49). His best-known works in this form are the* Military Polonaise, *the* Heroic Polonaise, *and the* Serbian Polonaise.

⑪ *Avant-garde composer Arnold Schoenberg (1874–1951).*

⑫ *Wolfgang Amadeus Mozart (1756–91). He wrote a full-fledged sonata at seven, a symphony at eight. His ear was so sensitive that he could perceive when a violin was tuned an eighth of a note too low.*

⑬ *These* Rasoumovsky Quartets *(1806) were commissioned by Count Rasoumovsky. Reflecting Beethoven's volatile moods at this time, the music is sometimes agitated, sometimes filled with an almost religious ardor.*

⑭ *Gioacchino Rossini (1792–1868), known for his versatility.*

⑮ *Franz Schubert (1797–1828), who also wrote fifteen string quartets.*

⑯ *Bagatelle. Beethoven wrote several bagatelles for the piano.*

⑰ *Etude; Chopin wrote twenty-four etudes which are also genuine works of art.*

⑱ *Erik Satie (1866–1925), who supported himself as a hack pianist in the Montmartre section of Paris. He wrote a famous jazz ballet* Parade.

⑲ *Robert Schumann (1810–56), who married Clara Wieck. When they first met, she was nine, he eighteen, and she was already being trained to become a concert pianist. Clara's father was so set against the marriage that the composer finally brought suit and won his case, allowing him to marry Clara at last.*

⑳ *George Friedrich Handel (1685–1759) wrote* The Harmonious Blacksmith. *There is another legend concerning the title, suggesting that it was invented by a publisher in Bath. He based it on a blacksmith who loved Handel's tune and sang it loudly as he worked, hence he was known in town as the "harmonious blacksmith."*

㉑ *Composer Franz Schubert (1797–1828), who also wrote a series of lovely piano "impromptus." One of them became famous in the motion picture* Sophie's Choice.

㉒ *Robert Schumann, who wrote* Papillons (Butterflies).

㉓ *Ludwig von Beethoven, composer of* Für Elise.

㉔ *Russia's best-known composer Peter Ilyich Tchaikovsky (1840–1893).*

㉕ *Claude Debussy (1862–1918), who wrote highly impressionistic works that included* La Mer *and* Afternoon of a Faun.

㉖ *German composer Robert Schumann (1810–56), who also wrote* Album für die Jugend (Album for the Young).

㉗ *Arthur Rubinstein (1887–1982). Seemingly indestructible, he appeared before the public until he was ninety.*

㉘ *Giuseppe Guarnieri (1638–1745). Like Avis, he was number two, but perhaps he tried harder.*

㉙ *François Couperin le Grand (1668–1733). His pieces are known for their structural perfection and variety of style.*

㉚ *1(e), 2(i) 3(g), 4(a), 5(b), 6(c), 7(h), 8(d), 9(j), 10(f).*

㉛ *1(e), 2(j), 3(b), 4(f), 5(g), 6(h), 7(a), 8(d), 9(i), 10(c).*

㉜ *One-time insurance executive and later composer Charles Ives (1874–1954).*

㉝ *John Cage (1912–   ).*

㉞ *Fritz Kreisler (1875–1962) is best-remembered for such shorter pieces as* Caprice Viennois, Liebesfreud, *and* Liebeslied.

㉟ *Vladimir Horowitz (1904–89), a moody genius who withdrew.*

㊱ *A statesman as well as a pianist, he was Ignace Paderewski (1860–1941).*

㊲ *André Watts (1946–). His first public appearance was at age nine with the Philadelphia Orchestra.*

Music for the Orchestra

M*any music lovers consider the symphony orchestra the greatest medium for transferring the ideas of the great composers into musical sounds. The symphony orchestras of today normally have 106 musicians, far short of Hector Berlioz' dream orchestra of 465. But with banks of stringed instruments, woodwinds, brass, and percussion, symphony orchestras can bring to life the ear-pounding fireworks of Peter Ilyich Tchaikovsky's* 1812 Overture, *or softly suggest the waves of the sea with Claude Debussy's tone poem* La Mer.

The giants among the world's composers have risen to the challenge of writing for symphony orchestras, and the most knowledgeable of musicians, the conductors, have been challenged to interpret their works. Can you rise to the challenge of answering some interesting questions on this subject?

1 Two nineteenth-century composers left famous symphonic works unfinished. The earlier (and more famous) actually wrote a ninth symphony after leaving his eighth incomplete. Can you name these composers?

2 In what city was America's first permanent symphony orchestra established, and what was its name?

3 This eighteenth-century harpsichordist, organist, and composer of concertos and oratorios wrote a suite of dances, airs, and fanfares for a royal water pageant on the Thames. It is one of his most popular works. Can you name the composer and this work?

4 If you have ever attended a graduation ceremony, you probably heard a piece of stately orchestral music called *Pomp and Circumstances*. Who is the composer of this work?

5 An American composer, who died in 1990 at age ninety, wrote three great orchestral works for the ballet: *Appalachian*

Spring, Billy the Kid, and *Rodeo*, based on American folk melodies. Who was he?

6 The person who had the greatest single influence on the art of conducting symphony orchestras was an Italian who was summoned to the conductor's podium in a last-minute emergency in Rio de Janeiro on June 30, 1886. After his sensational beginning, this cellist-turned-conductor led great orchestras for almost seventy years. Name him.

7 If one computed the performances of his work, his commissions, honors, and other forms of recognition, this composer could well be the most successful composer of the twentieth century. His *Spring Symphony* received standing ovations at its premieres. Name him.

8 Name the prolific German composer, the most renowned member of a large family of musicians, who wrote the Brandenberg Concertos in 1750.

9 When this composer died in 1937, most of the nation's music critics applauded his popular songs, but thought little of his serious works: one opera, a piano concerto, a rhapsody with jazz motifs, and an impressionistic Parisian suite. Who was this Brooklyn-born musician?

10 One unique and frequently played symphony is interpreted by its composer as follows: "A young musician of morbid sensibility and ardent imagination poisons himself with opium in a fit of amorous despair," causing "the strangest visions," which are "translated in his sick brain into musical thoughts and images." Name the composer and his symphony.

⑪ Can you name the composer of the *Bachianas Brasileiras,* a suite which attempted to fuse the style of Bach with elements of Brazilian folk music?

⑫ A number of symphonies have "names." Match these works in the column on the left with the composers at the right.

Work	Composer
1. *Eroica*	(a) Joseph Haydn
2. *Surprise Symphony*	(b) Gustav Mahler
3. *Great C Major Symphony*	(c) Felix Mendelssohn
4. *Winter Dreams Symphony*	(d) Roy Harris
5. *Giant Symphony*	(e) Robert Schumann
6. *Folk Song Symphony*	(f) Ludwig von Beethoven
7. *Prague Symphony*	(g) Franz Schubert
8. *Leningrad Symphony*	(h) Dmitri Shostakovich
9. *Reformation Symphony*	(i) Wolfgang Amadeus Mozart
10. *Rhenish Symphony*	(j) Peter Ilyich Tchaikovsky

How well do you know musical terms? Test yourself by answering the following questions.

13 Give the technical name of a form developed in the sixteenth and seventeenth centuries in which a group of solo instruments is set against the rest of the orchestra. It was the predecessor of the concerto.

14 What is the musical term for a short orchestral interlude performed between the acts of an opera or play to denote the passage of time?

15 Technically, what would you be listening to if you heard a dreamy piece of music suggesting night?

16 What does one call the technique of stating a theme and then subjecting it to a series of harmonic, rhythmic, and melodic alterations?

17 What is the term for a potpourri of melodies played by an orchestra? A famous Walt Disney film had this name.

18 What is the name given to orchestral music that tells a story or describes a mood?

19 Explain the controversial twelve-tone system used by such modern composers as Arnold Schoenberg (1874–1951).

⓴ Composers often give colorful names to their music for symphony orchestras. Match the works on the left with the composers on the right.

Work	**Composer**
1. *Fanfare for the Common Man*	(a) Manuel de Falla
2. *Enigma Variations*	(b) Hector Berlioz
3. *The Isle of the Dead*	(c) George Gershwin
4. *The Damnation of Faust*	(d) Aaron Copeland
5. *Academic Festival Overture*	(e) Serge Prokofief
6. *The Hungarian Fantasy*	(f) Franz Liszt
7. *Nights in the Gardens of Spain*	(g) Johannes Brahms
8. *An American in Paris*	(h) Sergei Rachmaninoff
9. *Peter and the Wolf*	(i) Sir Edward Elgar
10. *Till Eulenspiegel's Merry Pranks*	(j) Richard Strauss

⓴ This British composer is a brilliant orchestrator who is perhaps best known for the background music in such notable English films as *Hamlet* and *Henry IV*. He is also known for a cantata, *Balshazzar's Feast*. Name him.

⓴ One of the "Mighty Five" of Russian composers is best known for his unusual suite for orchestra based on unrelated episodes in *The Arabian Nights*. Who is the composer, and what is the title of this work?

23 One of the most original and innovative of twentieth-century orchestral works was inspired by a vision of a pagan rite in which a young girl dances herself to death. What is the name of this ballet, now often performed as a concert piece, which has sections entitled "The Fertility of the Earth" and "The Sacrifice," and who is the composer?

24 When students of music see a list of works in which the individual compositions are given an identifying number followed by the letter "K," they immediately know the name of the composer. Who was he?

25 Although he was French, this composer had a strong affinity for Spain. Some of his best works, including *Rhapsodie Espagnole*, reflect the Spanish scene with great affection and fidelity. Name the composer.

26 It has been said of this composer that "He is Finland in music; and he is Finnish music." His orchestral work *Finlandia* has been an eloquent voice for a land and its people. Who was the composer?

27 Well into the nineteenth century conductors wore articles of formal apparel that hindered their work. In Russia, Czar

Alexander II kindly allowed conductors to remove one of them so that the pages of the music could be turned more easily. Can you guess what they were wearing?

28 This composer wrote an orchestral suite that contains the most widely performed and celebrated piece of wedding music. Name the work and the composer.

29 A Russian composer's last work for orchestra was based on the myth of Prometheus. The composer planned to combine colored lights with the music and invented a special color-keyboard, which projected colors on a screen, synchronized with the music. Who was the composer?

30 A Soviet composer of Armenian birth is best known for a patriotic folk ballet called *Gayane* (or *Gayaneh*). It is also admired by concert audiences for two suites of twelve dances. One of these pieces, *Saber Dance*, became a popular hit in the United States, being arranged for jazz ensembles. Who was this composer?

31 Well-known for a "great zoological fantasy" called *The Carnival of Animals*, this French composer wrote every kind of music in great quantities: symphonies, chamber music, operas, chorales, ballet music, organ and piano music, and songs. Name him.

32 Before the conductors began using a baton early in the nineteenth century, a more common object was used to wave before the musicians. Can you guess what it was?

33 This Russian composer's ballet, *The Age of Steel* (1927), was his first attempt to put Soviet ideals into music. In 1948, however, when the Soviets began to denounce composers who wrote modern, intellectual music, he boldly stated: "They should stick to politics and leave music to the musicians." Name him.

34 The composer in the previous question wrote a delightful orchestral fairy tale that uses a narrator. Also, the flute, oboe, clarinet, and horns represent various animals. Can you name the composition and two of the animals represented?

35 This composer was remarkably adept at musical pictorialism, painting pictures with sounds. His three symphonic poems, *The Fountains of Rome*, *The Pines of Rome*, and *Roman Festivals* are frequently performed. Who is he?

36 Another Russian composer wrote a satirical orchestral work for a ballet called *Age of Gold*. This attempt in dance to satirize capitalism was complicated and confusing, but the music was highly praised. Who is the composer?

37 He became the staff pianist at the Radio City Music Hall at eighteen, and at twenty-one he was conducting the radio symphony of station WOR. In 1931 Leopold Stokowski and the Philadelphia Orchestra performed his *Chorale and Fugue in Jazz*. He also wrote *Cowboy Rhapsody*, *Latin-American Symphonette*, and *A Lincoln Legend*. Name him.

38 One of the world's most popular composers of waltzes was the son of one of Vienna's earliest waltz kings, who forbade his son to become a musician. The boy learned the violin secretly, and when his father deserted the family, he began studying openly. His wife inspired him to write *Wine, Women, and Song* and *Artist's Life*. Who was he?

39 An extraordinary pianist wrote one of the most frequently played short works for orchestra. It is an unbridled, demonic depiction of an episode in the Faust legend, highlighted by a wedding at a village inn. What is the name of this piece, and who was the composer?

40 This German composer left his homeland in 1935 when the Nazis came into power. His two best-known works are an opera and a symphony, both with the same title, named for a German religious painter. What is the name of the composer and his well-known pair of works?

41 Though he left his homeland forever at the outbreak of the Russian Revolution, this composer remained faithful to the holidays, language, and customs of his native land. One of his best-known works is *Rhapsody on a Theme by Paganini*. Who was he?

42 A native of Czechoslovakia, he was invited to become director of the National Conservatory in New York, where he learned to love the native music of African-Americans and Indians. His best-known work is a symphony that incorporates American melodies. Name the composer and the orchestral work.

43 Born in Hungary on March 25, 1881, he seemed to have had almost a second birth in 1904 when he heard an eighteen-year-old servant girl singing a folksong. He began searching for these folksongs and collected more than 6,000 of them, using many of them in his orchestral works. Who was he?

44 When one sees French cancan dancers in a sprightly routine, one composer will likely come to mind. He perfected the frothy style that epitomized the reckless fun of a particular time in Paris. He also wrote operas and operettas. Who was this composer, and what is the name of the suite containing his famous "cancan" section?

45 This eighteenth-century composer wrote a number of symphonies that had been given descriptive names: *London Symphony, Oxford Symphony, Miracle Symphony, Drum Roll Symphony,* and *Military Symphony.* Name the composer.

46 He boldly used dissonance in his orchestral works, invented instruments to simulate sounds of nature, including a wind machine and a thunder machine. The wind machine is used forcefully in the tone poem *Don Quixote.* Name him.

47 This composer of huge symphonies that attempted to express world philosophies was also a conductor. Although musicians recognized the conducting genius of this Austrian composer, some resented the physical and spiritual ordeals he subjected them to in an effort to achieve a perfect performance. Who was he?

48 One of the most successful tone poems ever written is *The Moldau,* one of a set of six national tone poems glorifying the composer's native land, Czechoslovakia, and collectively entitled *My Country.* Who was the composer?

49 He died at forty, depriving the world of the genius that had, in his brief career, already founded the romantic opera, created a new keyboard style, become the first traveling piano virtuoso, and blazed new trails as a conductor of orchestras. Name him.

50 This former Russian army officer wrote only one significant work for the orchestra, a frequently presented orchestral fantasy that is an eerie musical picture of the witches' sabbath that takes place on a mountain top at midnight on Saint John's Eve. Name the composer and his famous work.

51 Born in Bonn, Germany, he wrote nine symphonies and five piano concertos. At eight years old he made a debut as a concert pianist (though his father advertised that he was only six). At seventeen he played the piano for the great Mozart, who was not impressed until he heard him improvise on an assigned theme, commenting: "You will some day make a great noise in the world." Name him.

52 Called the national hero of Norway, he attempted to embody his country and its people in music. His best-known orchestral work is *Concerto in A Minor for Piano and Orchestra* (1868). Name him.

53 What composer is often said to be the originator of the symphony?

54 Which two instruments in the symphony orchestra are the most ancient?

55 Which section of the symphony orchestra is the hardest-working, carrying the major burden for the orchestra? Why?

56 This composer of operas is perhaps best known for a stirring orchestral overture once used as the opening theme of a radio and television show. He was also known for his wit by his contemporaries. When a young composer came to play two new piano compositions for him, he listened to the first and quickly said, "I like the other one better." Who was the composer?

57 Once, as an orchestra played a symphony of this Austrian composer, the musicians dropped out, one by one, each blowing out the candle by his music stand. Finally, only two violins and the composer-conductor were left. Then the violinists departed. Give the title of this aptly named symphony and the composer.

58 Name the eighteenth-century Italian composer/conductor who took a group of young girls in the Piéta, a school for orphans in Venice, and molded them into an admired orchestra for which he wrote many compositions.

59 The prolific composer in the preceding question wrote more than 400 concertos, over a hundred major choral works, and forty operas. His best-known orchestral work is in four parts, depicting the changes in nature through-out the year. Name it.

60 This composer, who had perfect pitch and could identify any note he heard, one day passed a pet shop and heard a starling sing the exact notes of a theme from his own *Piano Concerto in G Major*. He was so astonished and delighted that he bought the bird. Who was this composer who included in an opera a character who caught birds for a living?

The world of orchestral music has a number of outstanding conductors presently on the scene. Can you give their names from the following brief descriptions?

61 First, a conductor who was born in India and has had a long joint tenure conducting the Israel Philharmonic and the New York Philharmonic.

62 Born in Japan, he has had a distinguished career with the Boston Symphony.

63 A native of England, he conducted the BBC Orchestra in some memorable concerts before becoming conductor of the Toronto Symphony in 1975.

64 Although he is the artistic director at the La Scala in Milan, this conductor holds important positions with the London Symphony and the Vienna Philharmonic and is also a frequent conductor with American orchestras.

65 National telecasts from the Metropolitan Opera House in New York have made this conductor familiar to millions.

66 Identify these great conductors from the past from brief descriptions. First, this German conductor was born Bruno Schlesinger, but changed his name. He is especially noted for his interpretations of Mozart with the Berlin Philharmonic.

67 The first British-born conductor to achieve world-wide fame, he was the son of a wealthy manufacturer of pharmaceutical products. A celebrated wit, he once told a soprano that her voice reminded him of a cart coming downhill with the brake on. Name him.

68 He brought a new aura of glamor to the world of conducting in his long tenure as head of the Philadelphia Orchestra. He constantly retouched musical scores, saying "Beethoven and Brahms did not understand instruments." Name him.

69 This stirring overture, written in 1880, incorporates salvos by large artillery pieces. At the end, the peals of church bells contrast with the cannon shots. Name the composer and his deafening overture.

Answers

① *Franz Schubert (1797–1828) and Anton Bruckner (1824–96).*

② *New York, The Philharmonic. It was established in 1842, the same year that saw the creation of the Philharmonic in Vienna.*

③ *George Friderich Handel (1685–1759),* The Water Music *(1717). A similar suite by Handel is* The Royal Fireworks Music *(1749).*

④ *Sir Edward Elgar (1857–1934), an English composer.*

⑤ *Aaron Copeland (1900–90), who is also noted for* Lincoln Portrait, *for narrator and orchestra. It incorporates Stephen Foster songs as well as folksongs.*

⑥ *The great maestro, Arturo Toscanini (1867–1957). He had a long career as conductor of The New York Philharmonic and the NBC Symphony.*

⑦ *Benjamin Britten (1913–76), who was prominent among composers of opera, chamber music, and works for the orchestra.*

⑧ *Johann Sebastian Bach (1685–1750). Bach was also prolific in the siring of children. His first wife bore him seven children, his second wife thirteen. Three of his sons, Wilhelm, Karl, and John, were fine musicians and composers.*

⑨ *George Gershwin (1898–1937), composer of* Rhapsody in Blue, *which one critic calls "the best-loved and most frequently heard serious American work in the entire literature for orchestra."*

⑩ *Hector Berlioz (1803–69), who wrote* Symphony Fantastique, *a work of demonic energy and strident sounds.*

⑪ *Heitor Villa-Lobos (1887–1959), a largely self-taught Brazilian composer.*

⑫ *1(f), 2(a), 3(g), 4(j), 5(b), 6(d), 7(i), 8(h), 9(c), 10(e).*

⑬ *Concerto grosso. Established by Arcangelo Corelli, it was further developed and extended by Vivaldi, Handel, and Bach.*

⑭ *Intermezzo. The most famous are those by Mascagni in* Cavalleria Rusticana.

⑮ *A nocturne. Orchestral nocturnes in early classical music, called* notturno, *were written by Haydn.*

⑯ *Variations. The theme may be created by the composer, as in Bach's* Goldberg Variations, *(named for one of Bach's students) or it may be borrowed as in Brahms'* Variations and Fugue on a Theme of Handel.

⑰ *Fantasia. An example is Ralph Vaughan Williams'* Fantasia on Christmas Carols.

⑱ *Program music. Claude Debussy and Richard Strauss were masters of this form.*

⑲ *Rather than the harmonic progressions used by classical composers, Schoenberg used the twelve-tone chromatic scale (the white and black keys on the piano), arranged in a set sequence (or row), creating music that is unfamiliar in sound and structure.*

⑳ *1(d), 2(i), 3(h), 4(b), 5(g), 6(f), 7(a), 8(c), 9(e), 10(j).*

㉑ *William Walton (1902–   ). He was knighted in 1951 for his achievements.*

㉒ *Nicholas Rimsky-Korsakov (1844–1908), who wrote* Scheherazade. *Two other excellent orchestral works by this composer are* Capriccio Espagnol *and* Russian Easter Overture.

㉓ *The ballet is* Le Sacre du Printemps, *or* The Rite of Spring *(1913), by Igor Stravinsky (1882–1971).*

㉔ *Wolfgang Amadeus Mozart (1756–91). In 1862 a Viennese scholar, Ludwig von Köchel, catalogued Mozart's many com-*

positions. Since then, each work is catalogued by a number and "K."

㉕ *Maurice Ravel (1875–1937), who also wrote the popular* Bolero, *based on a Spanish dance.*

㉖ *Jean Sibelius (1865–1957). He also wrote* Tapiola, *a scenic tone picture of Finland.*

㉗ *White gloves.*

㉘ *Felix Mendelssohn (1809–47), who wrote* A Midsummer Night's Dream. *It was originally written as additional music for a performance of a play by Shakespeare.*

㉙ *Alexander Scriabin (1872–1915), an innovative composer who was willing to use new technology.*

㉚ *Aram Khatchaturian (1903–78). He was given the Lenin Prize for his ballet* Spartacus *in 1954.*

㉛ *The highly versatile Camille Saint-Saëns (1835–1921).*

㉜ *A rolled piece of paper, perhaps a sheet of music when it was first used by a conductor.*

㉝ *Serge Prokofiev (1891–1953). He also wrote the ballet* Romeo and Juliet, *seven symphonies, and five piano concertos.*

㉞ Peter and the Wolf *(1936). The flute (bird), oboe (duck), clarinet (cat), and horns (wolf).*

㉟ *Ottorini Respighi (1879–1936), who also wrote the opera* The Sunken Bell, *performed at the Metropolitan in New York in 1932.*

㊱ *Dmitri Shostakovich (1906–75). He also wrote the satirical ballet called* The Bolt.

㊲ *American composer/conductor Morton Gould (1913–   ).*

㊳ *Johann Strauss II.*

㊴ Mephisto Waltz *(1861) by Franz Liszt (1811–86).*

㊵ *Paul Hindemith (1895–1963). He wrote* Mathis der Maler, *the title of both the opera and the symphony, about Matthias Grünewald, the painter.*

㊶ *Serge Rachmaninoff (1873–43), who became an American citizen shortly before his death.*

㊷ *The composer is Antonin Dvořák (1841–1904).* From the New World *(or* New World Symphony*) is the name of the work. Even when he used American motifs, he gave them a Slavic flavor and personality.*

④③ *Béla Bartók (1881–1945). He was well known for his* Concerto for Orchestra, *which he wrote for the conductor Serge Koussevitzky.*

④④ *Jacques Offenbach (1819–80), who wrote the sprightly* La Vie Parisienne.

④⑤ *Composer of 104 symphonies, Franz Joseph Haydn (1732–1809).*

④⑥ *Richard Strauss (1864–1949), who also wrote the program symphonies,* Domestic Symphony *and* Alpine Symphony.

④⑦ *Gustav Mahler (1860–1911), who bridged the nineteenth-century style and the moderns.*

④⑧ *Bedrich Smetana (1824–84), considered the founder of modern Czechoslovak music.*

④⑨ *A forerunner of Wagner, Karl Maria von Weber (1786–1826).*

⑤⓪ *Modest Mussorgsky (1839–81), who wrote* A Night on Bald Mountain *and* Pictures at an Exhibition. *He also wrote the opera* Boris Godunov.

⑤① *The legendary Ludwig von Beethoven (1770–1827).*

⑤② *Edvard Grieg (1843–1907). He also wrote the incidental music for the play*

Peer Gynt, *and later created two orchestral suites from the music.*

㊾ *Franz Joseph Haydn (1732–1809). Most music historians now believe, however, that no one person can be given this honor because the symphony is a product of a long course of development.*

㊴ *The drum and the flute.*

㊶ *The stringed instruments play more than any other section in the orchestra because they have a breadth of pitch-range not equalled by the woodwinds or brass. Thus composers of symphonies rely primarily on the strings.*

㊹ *Gioacchino Rossini (1792–1868), still best known for the* Overture to William Tell, *the theme for the* Lone Ranger *radio and television show.*

㊷ Farewell Symphony *by Franz Joseph Haydn (1732–1809).*

㊸ *Antonio Vivaldi (1675–1741). He composed violin concertos, sonatas, and operas.*

㊾ The Four Seasons.

㉜ *Wolfgang Amadeus Mozart (1756–91). The bird-catching character is Papageno, in* The Magic Flute.

⑥⑴ *Zubin Mehta (1936–).*
He resigned as conductor of the New York Philhar-
monic in 1991.

⑥⑵ *Seiji Ozawa (1935–),*
known for his graceful movements with a baton.

⑥⑶ *Andrew Davis*
(1944–), who has conducted orchestras all over
the world.

⑥④ *A much-traveled conductor, Claudio Abbado (1933–).*

⑥⑤ *The popular and personable American, James Levine (1943–).*

⑥⑥ *Bruno Walter (1876–1962). He was conductor of the New York Philharmonic from 1947–50.*

⑥⑦ *Conductor/impresario Sir Thomas Beecham (1879–1961).*

⑥⑧ *Leopold Stokowski (1882–1977). He also conducted the New York Symphony Orchestra from 1944–45.*

⑥⑨ *Peter Ilyich Tchaikovsky (1840–93), composer of* Overture, 1812.

Architecture

T*o create buildings that are both useful and beautiful is the aim of the architect; therefore, no other art is more closely related to basic human needs. Architecture is also a blending of creative imagination and technical skill. We still marvel at the abilities displayed hundreds of years ago by the creators of the Egyptian pyramids, the great temples at Karnak, the Acropolis in Athens, and the cathedral at Chartres. As our civilization has progressed to higher technical advances, architects have been freed to create soaring structures of glass and steel.*

Let's see how you fare on this journey from pyramids to skyscrapers.

We'll start with two-part questions

about some of the world's greatest architectural gems, erected in antiquity.

❶ Completed in 27 B.C. as a temple to the gods, this massive structure encloses a remarkably large space whose only light source is the central hole in its famous cupola. (a) What is it called, and (b) where is it?

❷ The Pont du Gard, erected in the first century B.C., is a triumph of Roman engineering. Spanning more than eighty-two feet across a river, it is made up of uncemented blocks. (a) What is its function, besides serving as a bridge and (b) where is it?

❸ In southwestern Iraq there are huge, multistoried brick structures resembling terraced pyramids. Religious in purpose, they were thought of as "stairways from Heaven." (a) What are these structures called, and (b) can you think of the name given to such a structure in the Bible, by which the people attempted to reach Heaven?

❹ Near Salisbury, eighty-three miles west of London, is a ring of huge stones which were set up in a precise design between three to five thousand years ago. (a) What is the structure called, and (b) what do scientists now believe was its purpose or use?

5 A Roman invention, this design expanded a theater into an amphitheater by placing two theaters face-to-face to enclose an open arena. It was used for sporting events and cruel games with captured slaves and Christians. (a) What is this structure called, and (b) where is the largest example located?

6 One of the great underground architectural oddities, begun during the Period of Persecution of Christians in Rome, consists of a series of chambers and tunnels. (a) What are they called, and (b) what was their original purpose?

Let's see what you know about famous architects who are remembered for innovative masterpieces.

7 The piazza in front of Saint Peter's Church at the Vatican in Rome is designed in a vast oval, embraced by colonnades that are joined to the facade of the Cathedral. It was built during the years 1656–67. Who was the architect?

8 Who designed Saint Paul's Cathedral, an impressive form on the London skyline, noted for its huge dome?

9 The Kaufmann House (called "Fallingwater"), built in Bear Run, Pennsylvania, in 1936, makes use of a special setting in a very original way, as does this architect's winter quarters and workshop, Taliesin West (1938), near Phoenix, Arizona. Who is this architect?

⑩ The Federal Reserve Bank Building in Minneapolis is a daring "tension structure." The architect was Gunnar Birkets (1925–). Can you guess how this bold type of design, using the principles of the suspension bridge, can save much space in the future?

⑪ It took 20,000 laborers to build this beautiful, white marble mausoleum, a "monument to love," built in 1630–52 by the Emperor Shahjahan in memory of his second wife, who bore fourteen children and died in childbirth. Can you name the building?

⑫ Can you name the architect of a beloved Paris landmark that looks to some viewers like an oil refinery or an ocean liner, and was bitterly criticized when it was opened in 1977?

⑬ A present from a grateful king, this imposing palace was granted to the Duke of Marlborough in 1704 following his military victories in the Low Countries. The great statesman Winston Churchill was born here. What is the name of this famous British landmark?

⑭ This ultra-modern housing complex designed for the World's Fair, Expo '67, is made up of a nest of box-like units and has a bold, sculptural look. What is it called?

15 First used as a Christian church, then as a Moslem mosque, and finally as a secular museum, can you name this building in Istanbul, known for its huge and beautiful dome and the mosaics that decorate its inside walls?

16 A Spanish architect, whose works are primarily found in Barcelona, occupies a unique position in modern architecture. He has no predecessors and no successors. He produced a wide variety of works, but his crowning achievement was the bizarrely beautiful Church of the Sagrada Familia, still unfinished. It occupied him from 1884 until his death in 1926. Who is he?

17 What is the tallest building in the world, and where is it located?

18 Built for King George IV in 1784–87 as a backdrop for the royal pursuit of pleasure by the seaside, this "Indian Gothic" structure has Islamic domes, minarets, and screens. What is this building called? In what English city is it located?

19 In the year 785 the building of one of the world's most beautiful mosques was begun in Spain. Built later within the huge space of the mosque is a Christian cathedral, and the conjunction of the Christian altars with Moorish arches makes severe, but striking contrasts. In what city in Spain is it located?

20 Architecture has its own special terminology. Can you match the following definitions and terms?

Definition	Term
1. Roofed, open gallery overlooking courtyard	(a) rose window
2. Set of columns at regular intervals	(b) buttress
3. Triangular roof gable in classical architecture	(c) colonnade
4. Large hemispherical roof or ceiling	(d) dome building
5. Central block in an arch	(e) facade
6. The front of a building	(f) keystone
7. Projecting structure, supporting wall or building	(g) capital
8. Large circular stained glass window	(h) loggia
9. Upper member of a column	(i) vault
10. Arched masonry structure, usually forming a ceiling or roof	(j) pediment

21 The Banqueting Hall, Whitehall, erected in London in 1619–22, is one of the few remaining parts of Whitehall Palace. King Charles I passed through this room on his way to the scaffold in the street, where he was beheaded on January 30, 1649. What famous architect designed this building?

22 In the sixteenth century, when Pope Julius decided to build the greatest church in the world as the site of Saint Peter's Basilica in Rome, this architect was chosen along with Raphael and Bramante. He was the architect from 1547 until 1564 and conceived the great high dome—140 feet in span—that was necessary to balance the overall width. Do you know his name?

23 In the early fifteenth century the last of the great cathedrals in Italy, Santa Maria del Fiore in Florence, had remained unfinished for fifty years. No one knew how to support the weight of such a high roof. This architect, after studying the great dome of the Pantheon, conceived of a vault with an eight-sided dome, with deep, solid stone ribs at the corners and intermediate ribs to give it strength. It was used in many other buildings in Florence. Can you name the architect?

24 He studied architecture before the American Revolutionary War and spent much time in Europe before conceiving for

America a new kind of building. He wanted to give the ancient ideals of Greece and Rome new, creative expressions to fit new needs. His first design for a public building was the State Capitol at Richmond, Virginia. As president of the United States, he is thought to have influenced the architectural styles in Washington, D.C. What is his name?

㉕ As a sixteenth-century Italian architect, he was given the task of designing a new facade for the old regional palace at Vicenza. He solved it by surrounding the old great hall with an arcade in two stories, in which the bays were nearly square and the arches were carried on smaller columns. This bay design with its distinctive arches was given his name. Do you know it?

㉖ The three great pyramids of Giza (near Cairo) were built about 2700 B.C. When the Greek historian Herodotus visited the pyramids in the sixth century B.C., he gave them the Greek names by which they are still known: Cheops, Chephren, and Mycerinus. Of the three, which one is the largest?

㉗ In the Staatliche Museum, Berlin, is the magnificent restored Ishtar Gate (c. 575 B.C.). It is decorated with blue, beige, and green tiles and with pictures of sacred animals. What is its country of origin?

28 In the Museo Nazionale, Naples, is a mosaic, *The Battle of Alexander*, dating from the third to second centuries, B.C. It was originally found in a city completely covered by volcanic ash. What ancient city was this?

29 One of the most beautiful of ancient buildings, designed by architects named Ictinos and Callicrates, was at one time a Greek temple, at another a Christian church, and then a Turkish mosque. In 1687 a rocket hit the *cella* (storeroom), which was being used as an ammunition dump, blowing out the center of the building. Do you know the name of this building and its location?

30 Although warfare has destroyed many beautiful buildings, in World War II a bombing attack actually brought to light an architectural gem. The bombing of Palestrina, the modern successor of a medieval town that had been built over Praeneste, unearthed a great Roman temple. What is its name?

31 One of the most spectacular buildings devoted to leisure activities was erected in Rome about 215 A.D. The building had cathedral-like vaults that sprang up from thick masonry walls to heights of ninety feet. Beneath were a variety of spaces designed for intellectual as well as physical recreation. There was a capacity for 1,600 bathers, with pools of differing temperatures:

the *frigidarium* (cold), the *tepidarium* (warm), and the *calidarium* (hot). What is this building called?

32 In the fifth century B.C. a Milesian architect designed a checkerboard plan for laying out cities, consisting of a network of equally wide streets that intersected at right angles. At the center was a public building that housed markets and offices. One finds such a building in most ancient Greek cities. Do you know what it is called? And can you name the architect who gave his name to this city-planning scheme?

33 If you were looking for cathedrals that carry the baroque to an outrageous extreme, that use the decorative scheme of the *estipite* (or broken pilaster), that use high-relief sculpture from native traditions, and that display an overpowering use of gold, where would you go?

34 In 1851 a Great Exhibition was held in London's Hyde Park, and a famous building was erected. It was made of glass, set in a prefabricated iron building and considered far ahead of its time. Do you know the name of the building and its architect?

35 One of the great architectural gems of Italy is set in a grassy piazza, which enhances the brilliance of the marble exteriors of the group of buildings. Though the buildings are widely different, they are linked by the recurrent use of open arcades and inlaid marble decoration.

The Cathedral, Baptistry, and Tower are all superb examples of Romanesque architecture, but visitors come in great numbers to view the perilous angle of the *campanile* (bell tower). Where is this group of buildings located?

36 This building, built in 1920, decorates the skyline of a great city. It features a fanciful silver sunburst that derives from the Art Deco style. The top of the building provided the setting for the popular movie comedy *Ghostbusters*. Do you know the name of the building and its location?

37 What is the name of the art museum on Fifth Avenue in New York, designed by Frank Lloyd Wright, that features a large circular ramp on which art lovers can walk and look at an impressive collection of modern paintings?

38 The United States Pavilion at Expo '67 was dominated by a huge experimental building in the form of a prefabricated geodesic dome. Who was the designer of this building?

39 A native of Glasgow is considered to be the most inventive architect in Britain at the beginning of the twentieth century. He designed houses as well as the furniture and interior decoration. The overall interior effect is one of simplicity in the celebrated Hill House near Glasgow, with white walls and woodwork relieved by subtle colored decoration. Who was the architect?

40 One of the largest (440 rooms) and most beautiful of the chateaux of the Loire Valley in France was built by François I and overshadows Versailles in size. It is set in a forested area and was used as a "hunting lodge" for royalty. What is the name of this famous chateau of the sixteenth century?

41 This architectural marvel was built in the thirteenth and fourteenth centuries as the palace of the last Muslim rulers of Spain. From the outside it looks like a vast fortress, with bright red burnt-brick walls. Inside, it is a sumptuous palace of decorated rooms, courts, and formal gardens. What is the name of this great palace?

42 In 1964 Bertrand Goldberg Associates undertook a new type of urban housing. In order to avoid high land prices, twin concrete cylinders were designed to rise from the car parks, which spiral up to the eighteenth floor. Above them, wedge-shaped apartments fan out from a central core containing elevators and services, ending in rings of semicircular balconies. What is the name of this complex, and where is it located?

43 This architect was the leading exponent of the Art Nouveau style in Paris. His work is still enjoyed in the City of Light because of the wrought-iron entrances he designed for the Metro (the subway). Can you name him?

44 What is the name of the Neo-Gothic church, located at the head of Wall Street in New York City, that was designed by Richard Upjohn and completed in 1846?

45 The central plaza, or place, in this western European capital was destroyed in the siege of 1695. It was rebuilt in the traditional manner and is the last of the great public squares that is surrounded by guild houses. Where is it located?

46 This domed auditorium and cylindrical chapel at the Massachusetts Institute of Technology represents a courageous attempt to free modern buildings from boxlike forms. Built between 1953–55, its 1,500 tons rest at three points like a huge spinnaker on a pool of water. Who is the architect?

47 Grouped into a unified office and entertainment center, these buildings are placed around a fountained plaza and small garden in one of the most superb settings for American skyscrapers. The interiors are enriched by the allied arts of painting, sculpture, and mosaics. Can you name this center and give its location?

48 This famous design for a school building complex took its name from a distinctive German school for architects, founded in 1919. The plan encompassed an auditorium, dormitory, canteen, and offices in addition to departments and workshops. The most famous feature of the complex is the glass curtain walls. Name the architect and the group of buildings.

49 A famous rectangular slab, called *Unité D'habitation*, was a breakthrough in prefabricated construction. It was designed to house 1,000 people and has a frame into which apartment units are prefabricated and quite literally inserted. The familiar *brise-soleil* protects the occupants from excessive sun. Who was its renowned Swiss-born architect?

50 This noted designer and architect is now best remembered for a chair made of moulded plywood in a contemporary design. What is his name?

51 Born in China, he decided to become an architect when, at age sixteen, he saw his first skyscraper under construction. Two of his best-known works are the Mile High Center in Denver and the Library, which is shaped like a huge chair, at Cornell University, Ithaca, New York. Name him.

52 In 1932, in the middle of the Great Depression, seven British architects decided that they would be more successful working together. They pioneered the idea of group architecture in England, designing a series of imaginative buildings, including the Penguin Pool, at the Regent's Park Zoo in London. They also designed the renowned apartments at Highgate. What was the group called?

53 There were three distinctive styles of classical architecture, often distinguished by the different columns they used. Can you identify them from the following brief definitions?

(a) In about 338 B.C. this florid, highly decorated style, the most ornate of the three, became popular and was spread about Europe through Greek and Roman military domination.

(b) The most severely simple of the three types, this style was predominant until the end of the fifth century B.C.

(c) A style in between the simplest and the most decorative, it flourished briefly from the beginning of the fourth century B.C. until about 338 B.C.

54 Completed in 1976, this huge building has twin towers, each with 110 stories. It contains nine million square feet of office space, as well as the highest outdoor observation platform in the world. It was designed in 1962 by a team of architects headed by Minoru Yamasaki (1912–86). What is the name of this building?

55 In 1990 a controversial glass pyramid was erected atop a spectacular new entranceway to one of the world's great museums. It was designed by an American architect. Can you name him and the museum?

56 This famous city landmark, erected for the World's Fair of 1889, was an outstanding engineering achievement. It soared 984 feet into the air and was the world's tallest structure at the time. Do you know its name? If you do, you also know the name of the designer.

57 At 233 Broadway in Manhattan stands a famous building that was the tallest in the world from 1913–20. The Gothic-style Houses of Parliament in London were the inspiration for the architect, Cass Gilbert (1859–1934). It was built as the headquarters for a chain of "five-and-dime" stores. Can you name the building?

58 One of the nineteenth century's greatest engineering feats was a bridge designed by John Augustus Roebling and his son Washington. A New York landmark since its completion in 1883, it has a center span of 1,595 feet (more than fifty percent greater than any earlier bridge). Can you name it?

59 The facade of this Gothic cathedral, which is located in a western European capital, is noted for its geometric regularity and its blending of sculpture and architecture. Four or five master builders served as architects of this facade when the great church was built from

1200–50. It is balanced by two towers and a band of sculptured figures that tie the large rose window to the rest of the facade. What is this great Gothic masterpiece?

60 One of the joys of viewing great buildings is recognizing the architectural styles. Can you name the style described in the following brief definitions?

(a) Prevalent in western Europe from the twelfth through the fifteenth centuries, this style is characterized by pointed arches, ribbed vaulting, and flying buttresses.

(b) Flourishing in Europe from about 1550 to 1750, this style is characterized by elaborate and ornate scrolls, curves, and other symmetrical ornamentation.

(c) In France, during the third quarter of the nineteenth century, the naive self-confidence and exuberance of the newly rich classes was reflected in an abundance of decoration in architectural styles. The name for this style comes from the French word for "shell," and many shell-like forms are used in this style of architecture.

(d) This style of European architecture of the eleventh and twelfth centuries was based on the Roman style and was characterized by the use of round arches, thick, massive walls, and austere interiors.

(e) A style of decoration and architecture, first prevalent in the 1890s, with some of the best examples in America built during the 1930s. The style is characterized by the depiction of sinuous floral forms in a stylized, linear manner. The name for this style means "new art" in French.

61 Almost everything about this cathedral in France has inspired superlatives. Its nave has been called the "purest in France"; its stained glass, with a renowned special blue color, is called the finest anywhere, and the American author Henry Adams has called the south tower the "most perfect piece of architecture in the world." Can you identify this magnificent structure?

Answers

① *(a) The Pantheon, (b) located in Rome. It was an unparalleled structural feat for its time. It was restored by Hadrian after being damaged by fire in 80 A.D.*

② *(a) This beautiful bridge also served as an aqueduct and provided 100 gallons of water a day for each citizen of Nimes. (b) It is located near Nimes, in the Provence region of France.*

③ *(a) These are called ziggurats, and the best examples are found near the ruined cities of ancient Sumer: Ur, Warka, and Nippur. The ancient city of Borsippa, ten miles southwest of the modern city of Al Hillah, Iraq, has an excellent example. (b) The Tower of Babel, described in the Bible.*

④ *(a) Stonehenge, the mysterious primitive religious site, had a "calendric" use; that is, (b) it was used to mark the passage of days and seasons as the sun's rays at dawn coincided with certain spaces between the stones.*

⑤ *(a) A coliseum. (b) The largest example is the Colosseum in Rome, which seated 50,000 spectators for the opening performance in 80 A.D. of a reenactment of a naval battle—starring 3,000 participants—on its flooded arena floor.*

⑥ *(a) The Catacombs. (b) They were designed as cemeteries and places of worship for the burial of the Christian dead, many of them sainted martyrs. As many as 4,000,000 bodies were buried in the Roman catacombs. The tombs were dug out of a soft and granular limestone called* tufa stratum.

⑦ *Gianlorenzo Bernini (1598–1680), an architect, painter, and sculptor, one of the most brilliant artists of the Baroque era. He also worked on the interior of Saint Peter's, designing the magnificent bronze* baldacchino, *(1624–33), a canopy almost 100 feet high, placed beneath the cathedral's dome.*

⑧ *Christopher Wren (1632–1723). A mathematical genius and skilled engineer, whose work was praised by Sir Isaac Newton, he was asked by Charles II to restore the old Gothic church of Saint Paul. Within a few months, in 1666, the great fire of London destroyed the old structure, giving Wren the opportunity to do what he wanted: replace it with a new church, which was completed with remarkable speed from 1675–1710.*

⑨ *Frank Lloyd Wright (1867–1959). A great experimenter, he sought to develop an organic unity of structure, materials, and site. In the house called "Fallingwater," for example, a stream and a waterfall are incorporated into the design and landscaping.*

⑩ *In designing a "tension structure," the architect employs the principle used in suspension bridges. Great cables are strung between massive end towers to support a building by suspending it. This frees the open land below for other uses.*

⑪ *The Taj Mahal, erected in Agra, India, as a memorial to the emperor's wife, Mumtaz Mahal. It is said to have surpassed in beauty anything the world had seen, and the present-day cost is estimated at $100,000,000.*

⑫ *Renzio Piano (Italian) and Richard Rogers (British) are the innovative architects of the Pompidou Art Centre whose design won in a fierce competition. To gain as much space as possible inside, they placed stairs, elevators, escalators, ventilator shafts, hot-air pipes, etc., on the outside of the building.*

⑬ *Blenheim Palace, near London. It was designed by John Vanbrugh (1664–1726), who began as a writer of comic plays, turned to designing theaters, and later became a designer of elaborate palaces.*

⑭ *Habitat, Montreal. Moshe Safdie (1938–   ), an Israeli architect, designed the complex as an experiment in applying complete prefabrication to the building industry.*

⑮ *Hagia Sophia. The original fourth-century structure was gutted by fire in 532 A.D. and entirely rebuilt by Emperor Justinian the Great.*

⑯ *Antoni Gaudi (1852–1926), the son of a boilermaker of French descent. He is considered one of the great geniuses of modern architecture.*

⑰ *Sears Tower, Chicago, the work of the firm of Skidmore, Owings, and Merrill. Bruce Graham was in charge of design and Fazlur Khan the chief structural engineer. Erected between 1971–74, it has 110 floors and a height of 1,454 feet.*

⑱ *The Royal Pavilion in Brighton, England. John Nash (1752–1834) designed this unusual structure.*

⑲ *Cordoba, Spain. The mosque was converted into a cathedral after the city was captured by Fernando III in 1236. When this marvelous building was begun, Cordoba was the capital of Moslem Spain.*

⑳ *1(h), 2(c), 3(j), 4(d), 5(f), 6(e), 7(b), 8(a), 9(g), 10(i).*

㉑ *Inigo Jones (1573–1652), the architect for James I and Charles I.*

㉒ *Michelangelo Buonarroti (1475–1564). He prepared a wooden model of this design, but did not live to see it completed.*

㉓ *The ingenious engineer/architect, Filippo Brunelleschi (1377–1446).*

㉔ *Thomas Jefferson, who also designed buildings on the campus of the University of Virginia.*

㉕ *Andrea Palladio (1518–80). The terms "Palladian arch" and "Palladian motif" are still used.*

㉖ *The largest is the pyramid of Cheops, which is more like a mountain than a building. It is made up of more than six-and-a-half million tons of limestone, and each triangular face has five acres of surface.*

㉗ *Babylon. The famous gate dates from the New Babylonian Empire which* began in 625 B.C. Sacred processionals walked under the Ishtar Gate to celebrate the New Year.

㉘ The city of Pompeii, located near Sorrento and Naples, Italy.

㉙ The Parthenon, built as a temple sacred to Athena Parthenos. It was the first and largest of the buildings constructed on the Acropolis, high on a hill above the city of Athens, Greece.

㉚ The Sanctuary of Fortuna, east of Rome. The substructures for the temple are of concrete, a favorite Roman building material developed in the second century B.C. The Roman builders, in about 80 B.C., had converted the entire hillside into a great design symbolizing power and dominion.

㉛ The Baths of Caracalla; also included were gardens, shops, and libraries.

㉜ The Agora, the scene of much activity in most Greek cities and towns. Hippodamus was the designer, and his city-planning scheme was used widely.

㉝ To the Spanish and Portuguese colonies of Central and South America, as well as Mexico. The Cathedral of Mexico City is a riot of gilded wooden estipites and statues, centered on a painting of the Adoration of the Kings.

(34) *The Crystal Palace, the pride of Victorian England, designed by Joseph Paxton (1803–65).*

(35) *The Cathedral at Pisa, a white marble Romanesque structure that was begun in 1063. The tower continues to lean more dangerously each year.*

(36) *The Chrysler Building in New York City. The seventy-seven-story building was the world's tallest until the Empire State Building, with 102 stories, was built in 1931.*

(37) *The Solomon R. Guggenheim Museum, founded in 1937.*

(38) *The American architect and engineer Richard Buckminster Fuller (1895–1983) who invented the geodesic dome, the only large dome that can be set directly on the ground as a complete structure. Because of the design, the dimensions are not limited by the structural strengths of the materials.*

(39) *Charles Rennie Mackintosh (1868–1928), who was associated with the Art Nouveau movement as well as the Arts and Crafts movement in the early nineteenth century.*

(40) *The Château of Chambord. It is generally believed that its plan may have been suggested by Leonardo da Vinci, who was then living in France under the protection of the King.*

④ *The Alhambra, in Granada, begun under the leadership of Muhammad I al-Ghalib, the first ruler of the Nasrid dynasty (last of the Muslim dynasties in Spain).*

④ *Marina City, located on the river in downtown Chicago.*

④ *Hector Guimard (1867–1942). He designed some Metro entrances with fan-shaped pavilions, others with balustrades around them.*

④ *Trinity Church, which has a steeple 284 feet high.*

④ *The Grand Place in Brussels, Belgium. It is one of the most beautiful public squares in the world.*

④ *Eero Saarinen (1910–61), who designed the Kresge Auditorium and Chapel at the Massachusetts Institute of Technology in Cambridge, Massachusetts.*

④ *Rockefeller Center, a group of skyscrapers built on Fifth Avenue in New York City from 1929–40. It is simple in design and highly imaginative in urban approach and was designed by a team of architects headed by Henry Hofmeister, H.W. Corbett, and Raymond Hood.*

④ *Walter Gropius (1883–1969) designed the Bauhaus. The Bauhaus school curriculum included work with hand-tools and the study of nonrepresentational painting, but no technical study of either materials or structure.*

④⑨ *Charles Edouard Jeanneret (1887–1965), known by his architectural pseudonym, Le Corbusier. He designed this building, which was erected in Marseilles, France.*

⑤⓪ *Charles Eames (1907–78). He designed the Eames chair and won a first prize in 1940 in an Organic Design Competition conducted by the Museum of Modern Art.*

⑤① *I. M. Pei (1917–).*

⑤② *The Tecton Group.*

⑤③ *The styles are as follows: (a) Corinthian, (b) Doric, (c) Ionic.*

⑤④ *The World Trade Center, built on the southern tip of the island of Manhattan.*

⑤⑤ *The glass pyramid in the Cour Napoleon in Paris that allows orderly entrance into the Louvre Museum. It also houses underground book shops and cafes, located at the center of corridors leading to the various wings of the museum. It was designed by I. M. Pei.*

⑤⑥ *The famous Eiffel Tower, which offers a dazzling view of Paris. It was designed by Alexandre Gustave Eiffel (1832–1923).*

(57) *The Woolworth Building, completed in 1913, and still considered one of the most beautiful of the New York skyscrapers.*

(58) *The Brooklyn Bridge, which pioneered the use of caissons for working under water and the use of steel cables.*

(59) *Notre-Dame de Paris. Ingenious use of an arrangement of nine squares (three-times-three to illustrate the Trinity) makes the facade truly unusual.*

(60) *(a) Gothic, (b) Baroque, (c) Rococo, (d) Romanesque, (e) Art Nouveau.*

(61) *The Cathedral at Chartres, a pure masterpiece of medieval cathedral architecture, which took many years to perfect. One of the towers was erected in 1506, another, four hundred years earlier.*

Sculpture

Even our prehistoric ancestors delighted in trying to imitate natural objects in primitive sculpture, primarily using it to decorate weapons and utensils. Human figures were sculpted more than five thousand years ago in ancient Egypt. In the fourth century B.C. Greek sculptors, following their religious principles of idealizing nature and humanity, produced sculpture that would forever leave its mark on Western art. Sculpture was used to decorate the great cathedrals of the Middle Ages, and Renaissance geniuses like Michelangelo astounded the art world with their poetry in marble. In the nineteenth century Auguste Rodin took sculpture a giant step into the future.

If modern sculpture has degenerated, as some say, into experiments with new forms such as mobiles and new materials like plastic, it continues to be a vital part of the world of art. It's a vast subject, so let's get underway.

❶ Let's get warmed up with an easy question. One of the world's best-loved statues is a huge one, made of hammered copper sheets and placed on a stone pedestal in a harbor in 1886. For a two-parter: (a) name the statue, and (b) the Italian sculptor who created it.

❷ Do you have a clear mental picture of the statue in the above question? Good! (a) In which hand is she holding an object aloft? (b) What is the object?

❸ One of the earliest and most widely known portrait statues was of a queen. It was carved and painted in Egypt in the early fourteenth century B.C. Who was this queen with a long, delicate neck and sharp features?

❹ "Ugly" is the word for the sculptured animal and human figures that project from the rooftops of medieval churches. No, they were not put there to scare away evil spirits, but to perform a more practical function. Do you know (a) the generic name for these hideous carvings, and (b) their actual use?

5 Art historians have a theory that mankind's first artistic skill was sculpting, not painting. Can you think of a logical reason why this might be true?

6 One of the world's largest sculptures is the Great Sphinx of Giza located near Cairo, Egypt. It has a human head and the body of what animal?

7 It was a sculptor who first represented the Nativity Scene in art. Can you guess the approximate date of this work? (You won't guess a date in the B.C. era, of course.)

8 It may seem unkind to say, but the most amazing characteristic of the sculpture of one country is its monotony. For forty centuries it followed the same conventions and styles. What country was it?

9 One of the seven wonders of the ancient world was a gigantic tomb on the coast of Asia Minor, containing some magnificent sculptures. It was built for King Mausolus of Caria about 350 B.C. What word, still used today, comes from that king's name?

10 Originally part of the Parthenon in Athens, these masterpieces of sculpture are now in the British Museum. They are known by the name of the aristocrat who acquired them from the Turks and brought them to London. What are they called?

⓫ This great sculptor of ancient Greece scandalized the public by using a promiscuous courtesan named Phryne as the graceful, girlish model for his statue *Aphrodite of Arles.* Name him.

⓬ What well-known statue, one of the most popular in the Louvre, portrays a Greek goddess who is missing both arms?

⓭ Generally conceded to be the greatest of the Greek sculptors, he created the huge *Zeus of Olympia,* one of the seven wonders of the ancient world. In the fifth century B.C., he acted as a sort of Minister of Fine Arts to Pericles. Name him.

⓮ From about 800 to 50 B.C. an original and creative race of people lived in the Tuscany area of Italy. Their sculpture, particularly the bronze puppets depicting strange rituals and beliefs, is considered superior to the art of the Romans who conquered them. Were they (a) the Etnans, (b) the Etruscans, or (c) the Euboeans?

⓯ If there had been a *Guinness Book of World Records* in the fourth century B.C., this city would have held the record for bronze statues, with 3,785. Name the city.

16 One of the best-known groupings of religious sculpture is found in the "Royal Portal," an entrance to one of the world's most beautiful cathedrals, southwest of Paris. Is it located at (a) Chartres, (b) Chambord, or (c) Chenonceau?

17 In twelfth-century Italy, a father, a son, and a grandson glorified the family name in the world of sculpture. The father carved the magnificent baptistry at Pisa, mixing the Adoration of the Magi with the heroics of Hercules. What was their name? (Hint: the last name suggests the Italian word for "friend.")

18 One of the Florentine artists who created the Renaissance style in the early fifteenth century was commissioned to carve a marble singing gallery for the Florence cathedral. The exquisite finished work includes ten reliefs depicting children singing and playing instruments. Name him.

19 This major Renaissance sculptor detested working in bronze. He thought the building up of clay and wax models (from which the bronze is cast) was too easy and that direct carving in stone was the only method worthy of the great artist, whose purpose was liberating the forms hidden in a block of marble. Name him.

20 The great sculptor in the previous question created several statues of the Madonna holding the crucified Jesus. The three most famous are in the Castello Sforzesco (Milan), the Florence Cathedral, and Saint Peter's in Rome. (a) What is the name given to all three of these statues, and (b) which is the most famous?

21 We have already referred to *relief* type of sculpture. Can you (a) give the meaning of this term and (b) give one of the two basic types of this form?

22 One sculptor, who was brilliant in using relief sculpture, created the magnificent gilt bronze doors of the Baptistry in Florence. Michelangelo called them the "Gates of Paradise" because of their sculptured themes and great beauty. Name him.

23 There is a colossal statue of the young David in Florence that is known by art lovers all over the world. Another sculptor, who was the first to use live models for his religious subjects, did two other statues of David, one in stone and the better-known one in bronze, which was the first nude statue of the Renaissance. Name these two sculptors who used David as a subject.

24 A seventeenth-century sculptor captured the religious rapture of a saint in his *The Ecstasy of Saint Teresa*. The saint, in sacrifice to God, offers her heart to the golden arrow of

Divine Love, with which an angel inflicts on her a pain so fierce and yet so sweet that she longs for it to last forever. Who was the artist who captured this ecstatic moment?

25 Four great stylistic periods appeared successively in the art world, beginning in 1400: the Renaissance, Mannerism, Baroque, and Rococo. Identify the period and style from the descriptions that follow:

(a) An artistic style of the late sixteenth and early seventeenth centuries, that distorted such elements as scale and perspective for a special effect.

(b) A period in which artists tried to imitate nature in a realistic, more human way than the religion-centered medieval period had done. The human figure, avoided by medieval artists, became the sculptor's main subject. Among artists there was a great desire for knowledge, particularly in science.

(c) A style of art, developed in France in the early eighteenth century, which was characterized by elaborate, profuse designs intended to produce a delicate, but artificial, effect.

(d) A style of art characterized by grand theatrical effects and elaborate ornamentation.

26 As this great Italian sculptor became more nearsighted in his later years, he began leaving more of his work unfinished. A statue of a slave (1532) only partially emerges from a marble block. The artist liked the effect, believing it "spiritualized" the stone. Name him.

27 In the Abbey Church at Saint Denis in France is a sculptured monument that contains a human organ. The reliefs on the urn and base represent architecture, sculpture, music, and other arts to show that the honoree, Francis I, was a patron of the arts. (a) Try to guess which organ the monument contains, and (b) name the artist.

28 In sculptures that depict body forms, artists must be aware of the counterbalancing humans use to stay erect. For example, in a statue of the Virgin Mary holding the Child, she may sit with her back bent slightly backward to counterbalance the weight she holds. *Parla italiano?* (Do you speak Italian?) Give the word sculptors use to describe this technicality.

29 Certain Indian peoples of the northwest coast of North America had their own special form of sculpture. They carved and painted logs with symbolic animal faces and then erected them in front of their houses. What were these posts called?

30 In the Louvre there is a rough relief sculpture of a group of emigrants of all ages struggling forward in a painful stance. The artist, mainly known for satirical caricatures, worked in several media. Name him.

31 In 1877 a work called *Age of Bronze* was unveiled in an exhibition in Paris. It created a scandal because a nude young man seemed to come alive in bronze much more realistically than in statues by classical sculptors. The artist was to dominate the world of sculpture in the late nineteenth and early twentieth centuries. Can you name him?

32 Name three of the many masterpieces by the sculptor in the preceding question.

33 The above artist was so prolific that there are two museums devoted to his works in the country of his birth. Do you know where they are located?

34 An Impressionist painter, known for the ample female figures in his paintings, turned to sculpture late in life. His statue of a buxom woman, on one knee and holding a cloth in each hand, is called *The Washerwoman* and is owned by the Museum of Modern Art in New York. Who was this sculptor-painter?

35 Another famous sculpture by the above artist is a high-relief depiction of three nudes, somewhat obese by today's standards, being judged in a kind of mythological beauty contest by a young man. Can you name it?

36 This painter, the father of French Fauvism, studied sculpture at the École de Ville in Paris, and even in his first standing bronzes he distorted the proportions of the body. In sculpture, he is best remembered for a number of highly original and witty works. Name him.

37 Painters were greatly influenced by sculptors in the mid-nineteenth century. One Post-Impressionist who excelled in his colorful canvases of island peoples, was inspired by primitive wood sculptures. He also carved bas-relief sculpture in wood, which he painted in bright colors. Can you name him?

38 A French painter of ballet dancers and horse racing scenes was also a sculptor. His small bronzes of dancers have such titles as *Arabesque*, *The Little Ballet Dancer*, and *The Bow*. He also created a bronze grouping called *The Masseuse*, a realistic work depicting a woman receiving a massage. Name him.

39 Although Art Nouveau is primarily a movement in decoration, it is used strongly in an unusual memorial to Beethoven. The composer is shown on a throne in a fanciful setting, and the work is filled with symbols. Name the German sculptor who created it.

40 In 1909 a Romanian sculptor created an unusual portrait bust that was turned on its side and shaped like an egg, which, for the sculptor, symbolized the origin of life. He entitled the bust *Sleeping Muse* and sculpted a series of similar works that explored the "essence of things." Name him.

41 Another work by the artist in the previous question was carved from a block of gray-veined marble. An abstract shape, with all details eliminated, it somehow conveys the essence of a certain large aquatic mammal. What is this sea animal?

42 A renowned Italian painter of thin, elongated nudes turned to sculpture and created works that are closely akin to Cubism. Typical is *Female Head*, carved from a long, flat block of granular limestone. Name him.

43 A highly successful Swedish sculptor, popular in the United States, created the huge *Peace Monument* in Mexican onyx for the City Hall at St. Paul, Minnesota, in 1936. The work incorporates varying folklores from Ancient Greek to Scandinavian to Mayan. Name him.

44 This sculptor created one of the most ingenious funerary monuments of the twentieth century. It clearly expresses the personality of an English dramatist and wit who died in Paris and is buried at the Père Lachaise Cemetery. The sculptor combines Assyrian, Greek-Archaic, and Art Nouveau ingredients with great skill. Name (a) the artist and (b) the honored author.

45 Perhaps the most widely known of all modern artists, this painter began sculpting heads in 1905 with no instruction in the art. In 1924 he elicited the help of a friend, Julio Gonzalez, in his experiments in metal sculpture. His best-known work in that medium is a bronze and welded-iron sculpture entitled *Woman in the Garden* (1929–30). Name this Spanish artist.

46 In 1944 the artist in the preceding question created a seven-foot bronze figure in a modified classical style. This work, which somehow combines the Greek *Calfbearer* with the Christian *Good Shepherd* is poles apart from his Cubist sculpture. What is the name of this sculpture?

47 The work of this twentieth-century Lithuanian sculptor reflects both a tendency toward Cubism and an interest in primitive totem poles. His *Figure* is abstract, with two peering eyes and the torso made up of varied-sized open spaces. Name him.

48 After 1930 this French sculptor attempted to discover new forms of organic life and sculpt them in rounded marble shapes. Name this artist who imagined these new creatures.

49 A German sculptor constructed collages of three-dimensional objects, such as scraps, and ready-made objects, such as tools. One of his best known is a collage of painted wood and metal called *Fruits of Long Experience*. Name him.

50 The two preceding artists were a part of the Dada movement in Western European art. As strange as it may sound, this term does come from the usual first word a baby speaks. Aside from this baby-talk name, what characterizes Dadaism?

51 What is the largest piece of sculpture in the world? Hint: It has three prominent Americans sculptured in relief on the side of a mountain. Another hint: None of the three figures were presidents of the United States.

52 A British woman carved rounded, sometimes shell-like, natural objects out of Cornish elm. She had a rare talent for revealing all the beauty of color, grain and surface of her chosen material. Name her.

53 After a period of Surrealism, this Swiss sculptor turned his attention to painting and sculpting the human figure in new ways. A typical work is *The Chariot*, in the Museum of Modern Art in New York. It depicts a long, thin charioteer atop a simplified, abstracted chariot. Who was the artist?

54 A Venezuelan-American artist, who uses only her first name, does life-size figure sculpture using wood, plaster, synthetic polymer paint, and miscellaneous items. In *Women and Dog* she satirizes life of the '60s by depicting a group waiting to cross a New York street. They wear real clothes, and the base of the stiff-legged wooden dog supports a stuffed dog's head. Name her.

55 In the 1940s she experimented with all media; in the 1950s she began working in wood, constructing repetitions of cubic boxes, usually painted black. Her massive work in the Jewish Museum, New York, is entitled *Homage to 6,000,000*, a tribute to the victims of the Holocaust. Who is she?

56 He invented a new kind of sculpture, consisting of parts that move in response to air currents. His best-known sculpture is called *Lobster Trap and Fish Tale*. What is his name and what is this modern type of sculpture called?

57 This artist also did another type of abstract sculpture that had no moving parts. One of his statues, made of twisted wire, depicts the famous black dancer Josephine Baker. What is the name of this type of sculpture?

58 When he was only twenty-three, Daniel Chester French, one of America's best-known sculptors, was commissioned by the town of Concord, Massachusetts, to create a statue for the centenary of the Battle of Concord. It became an American classic. What was the statue called?

59 Some artists become associated with a certain type of subject matter, but no one more so than the French sculptor Antoine Louis Barye (1796–1875). He sculpted one type of animal over and over. What was it?

60 Every day thousands of New Yorkers pass beneath a pair of huge sculptured figures on either side of an ornamental clock, the work of Edward McCartan (1878–   ). In what building can you find this work of art?

61 Visitors to India will see countless statues of one subject: a figure with four arms, usually poised on one foot like a dancer. The figure is surrounded by a circular device. What does this figure represent?

62 A Renaissance artist, primarily known as a goldsmith, created a masterpiece called *Perseus with the Head of Medusa*, now in Florence. Name him.

63 The great American artist Augustus Saint-Gaudens (1840–1907) is best remembered for his large bronze relief sculpture in Boston, showing a young colonel on horseback, leading a regiment of black soldiers in the Civil War. The officer and his soldiers were the subject of a recent award-winning motion picture called *Glory.* Name him.

64 Although Chinese artists were creating beautiful bronze ritual vessels three thousand years ago, they did not begin sculpture as we know it until the fifteenth century. Near Beijing, nearly a mile of colossal statues from this period guard the approach to some famous tombs. Name them.

65 Frederic Remington (1861–1909), an American artist, produced a number of highly distinctive bronze statues on subject matter uniquely his own. What were his favorite subjects?

Answers

1 *(a)* The Statue of Liberty, *(b) Frédéric-Auguste Bartholdi (1834–1904). The statue was so immense that it required the services of the engineer Alexandre Gustave Eiffel (known for his famous tower in Paris) to erect it in place.*

② (a) The right, of course. You don't think the French would give us a statue that holds the (b) torch of liberty in the hand they call "gauche," do you?

③ The beautiful Queen Nefertiti, wife of King Akhenaton.

④ (a) Gargoyles (from an old French word for "throat"), and (b) to carry rainwater clear of the walls.

⑤ For primitive people, painting was a luxury, sculpture a necessity. They had to learn to carve stone and chip flint so that they could fashion tools. The next step was to create beautiful imitative objects used in worship.

⑥ A lion. The statue represents the god Harmakhis, a form of the solar deity, and serenely guards the entrance to the other world.

⑦ The manger scene, depicting the newborn Christ, the Virgin Mary, shepherds, and the Magi, was first represented in the fourth century as a carved relief on Christian Roman sarcophagi (stone coffins).

⑧ Egypt. The next time you see a group of Egyptian statues, note how similarly posed and static they appear.

⑨ The word is mausoleum, which means a stately or elegant tomb.

⑩ *They are the Elgin marbles, named for Lord Elgin, who brought them to England in 1801–03. Executed under the supervision of the great sculptor Phidias, they depict the triumph of civilization over barbarism.*

⑪ *Praxiteles, the fourth century* B.C. *Athenian sculptor whose choice of models raised eyebrows. He also claimed that Phryne inspired the first full-scale statue of the God of Love, the* Eros of Thespiai.

⑫ *Called the* Venus de Milo, *the date of its creation is controversial. In general form it belongs to a classical tradition that began early in the fourth century* B.C. *The twist of the body suggests a late Hellenistic creation, dating from the second or first century* B.C. *The bottom line: don't bite your fingernails.*

⑬ *Phidias, who was born about 500* B.C. *His great statues,* Zeus of Olympia *and* Athena Parthenos, *no longer survive.*

⑭ *(b) The Etruscans, also sometimes called the Etrurians.*

⑮ *Rome, Italy, the "Eternal City." It commemorated events with statues, showing the citizens' love of history and public records.*

⑯ *(a) Chartres, known for its profusion of fine sculpture. Chenonceau and Chambord are two of the beautiful chateaux of the Loire Valley in France.*

⑰ *Pisano. Nicola was the father, Giovanni the son, and Andrea the grandson.*

⑱ *Luca della Robbia (c.1400–82). This beautiful grouping of low-relief sculpture represents a movement in art away from the Gothic of the Middle Ages and toward a revitalized classical style of the Renaissance.*

⑲ *The brilliant Italian Michelangelo (1475–1564).*

⑳ *(a) They all have the title* The Pietà. *(b) The most famous is in Saint Peter's Church in the Vatican. It was damaged in recent years by a madman with a sledge hammer.*

㉑ *Relief is a type of two-dimensional sculpture set against a flat background. If the figures barely emerge from the background, it is called "low relief" (or* bas-relief*). If they emerge from their background at least one-half of their depth, it is an example of "high relief." Relieved?*

㉒ *Lorenzo Ghiberti (1378–1455). He was much less successful in his free-standing sculpture.*

㉓ *Michelangelo. He did one and Donatello (1377–1446) created two.*

㉔ *Italian sculptor/architect/painter Gian Lorenzo Bernini (1598–1680).*

㉕ *These periods, of course, overlap: (a) Mannerism (1520–1620), (b) Renais-*

sance (1400–1550), (c) Rococo (1720–80), and (d) Baroque (1600–1750).

㉖ *Michelangelo again. He also used this technique deliberately in the* Rondanini Pietà.

㉗ *(a) The heart of the king is preserved in the monument sculptured by (b) Pierre Bontemps (c.1507–70).*

㉘ *"Contrapposta."*

㉙ *Totem poles. These were emblems of clans within the tribe.*

㉚ *Honoré Daumier (1808–79), the sculptor of* The Emigrants.

㉛ *Auguste Rodin (1840–1917), considered by many one of the greatest of all sculptors.*

㉜ *Rodin's sculpture is by far the best known of any nineteenth or twentieth century artists. Almost everyone has seen pictures of* The Thinker, The Kiss, Monument to Balzac, The Old Courtesan, The Gates of Hell, *and* The Burghers of Calais.

㉝ *In Paris there is a Rodin Museum in a beautiful mansion on the rue de Varenne, where he worked until his death. Even the nearby Varenne Métro (subway) Station has a lifesize copy of his statue of Balzac. To see the house and* grounds he bought for himself, art lovers go out of Paris to the suburb of Meudon. A museum annex there houses many of his sketches and statuary.

㉞ *Auguste Renoir (1841–1919), perhaps better known for his paintings in soft, pastel colors.*

㉟ The Judgment of Paris, *in which the young shepherd is deciding who is the more beautiful: Juno, Aphrodite, or Pallas Athena.*

㊱ *Henri Matisse (1869–1954), who sculpted two important works, both owned by the Museum of Modern Art in New York:* The Slave *(1900–03) and* La Serpentine *(1909).*

㊲ *Paul Gauguin (1848–1903), who painted in Tahiti and the Marquesas Islands.*

㊳ *Edgar Degas (1834–1917). When his eyesight began to fail, Degas concentrated on sculpture.*

㊴ *Max Klinger (1857–1920), also known for his macabre etchings.*

㊵ *Constantin Brancusi (1876–1957), a shepherd boy turned artist.*

㊶ *A seal. Brancusi also sculpted abstractions of fish and parts of human torsos.*

④② *Amedeo Modigliani (1884–1920). His first one-man show in Paris was closed for indecency.*

④③ *Carl Milles (1875–1955), best known as a designer of fountains.*

④④ *(a) Sir Jacob Epstein (1880–1959), and (b) Oscar Wilde (1854–1900). Epstein is satirized, along with Gertrude Stein and Albert Einstein, in a well-known limerick:*
　There's a wonderful family called Stein,
　There's Gert and there's Epp and there's Ein;
　Gert's poems are bunk,
　Epp's statues are junk,
　And no one can understand Ein.

Anonymous

④⑤ *The prolific and innovative Pablo Picasso (1881–1973).*

④⑥ *Picasso called the sculpture simply,* Man with a Sheep.

④⑦ *Another cubist, Jacques Lipschitz (1891–1973).*

④⑧ *Jean Arp (1887–1966), who arrived at his sculptural style through Dadaism and Surrealism.*

④⑨ *Max Ernst (1891–　　), who was also influenced by the Dada Movement.*

(50) *Dadaism tried to abolish traditional artistic and cultural forms by satirizing them. The guiding principles of this kind of art were irrationality, chance, and intuition. Clifton Fadiman, an American wit, said that Gertrude Stein was the "mama of Dada."*

(51) *If you guessed Mount Rushmore, you were wrong. The prize goes to the sculpture of Jefferson Davis, Robert E. Lee, and Thomas "Stonewall" Jackson that fills 1.33 acres on the face of Stone Mountain, near Atlanta, Georgia. The sculpture, which took almost ten years to complete, was finished on March 3, 1972.*

(52) *Honored with the title "Dame," Barbara Hepworth (1903–   ).*

(53) *Alberto Giacometti (1901–66), known for his "thin man" bronzes.*

(54) *Marisol (1930–   ).*

(55) *The innovative Louise Nevelson (1900–88).*

(56) *Alexander Calder (1898–1976). Modern sculptures of this type are called "mobiles." Later, Calder placed small motors inside his art works. (Do you think they should be called "automobiles?")*

(57) *These stationary statues are called "stabiles." The name is not particularly log-*

ical, so don't apply the term to all statues that stay in place, such as Michelangelo's statues.

⑤⑧ The Minute Man. *French also sculpted the statue of Lincoln for the Lincoln Memorial in Washington. New Yorkers enjoy his four groups: Europe, America, Asia, and Africa, created for the facade of the New York Customs House near Battery Park.*

⑤⑨ *The combativeness of large wild cats, such as lions, tigers, and jaguars, endlessly fascinated Barye. Typical are* Lion Devouring a Crocodile *and* Lion and Snake.

⑥⓪ *Grand Central Station.*

⑥① *The figure of Siva, the post-Vedic god of Hindu mythology.*

⑥② *The Italian Benvenuto Cellini (1500–71), also known for his autobiography.*

⑥③ *The sculpture, begun in 1884 and completed in 1897, is a memorial to Colonel Robert G. Shaw. Another famous statue by Saint-Gaudens of a seated woman in a hood is known (confusingly) by three names:* Grief, Death, *and* The Peace of God. *This sculptor, who believed eccentricity was a plus for artists, once said: "What garlic is to salad, insanity is to art."*

㉞ *The Ming Tombs, guarded by a succession of statues of large animals and warriors.*

㉟ *The American West, primarily cowboys and Indians on horseback. One of his best works is* Bronco Buster.

European Painting

Europe has a long and rich heritage in the art of painting, and different countries and their artists have had particular periods of great glory. It was in Italy in the fifteenth and sixteenth centuries that the Renaissance had its heyday, led by Giotto, Botticelli, Leonardo, Michelangelo, Raphael, and Titian, among others. Rembrandt and Vermeer towered over the Dutch school in the seventeenth century. French painters, centrally placed between northern and southern Europe, absorbed the influences of other countries, but developed a strong individuality that kept them at the forefront from the seventeenth century onward. In the nineteenth century, the French Impressionists—Manet, Monet,

Pissarro, Renoir, and others—brought about astounding changes in the technique of painting. The Flemish painter Van Eyck, the Spanish painters Velasquez and Goya, and the British Gainsborough, Turner, and Constable all made important contributions. These few names merely begin a list of important European artists. How well do you know them?

❶ Before we tackle questions about painters and paintings, try your hand at matching the following definitions with these art terms.

Definition	**Term**
1. System used to create the illusion of three-dimensional space on a flat plane.	**(a)** pointillism
2. Painting that uses domestic and homey scenes as subject matter.	**(b)** chiaroscuro

Definition	Term
3. Pictures made by setting small colored pieces of stone, glass, etc., in mortar.	**(c)** composition
4. A medium for painting that uses water colors mixed with a gummy preparation.	**(d)** mosaic
5. Painting with dots of color.	**(e)** collage
6. A painting on three panels, usually serving as altar-pieces.	**(f)** fresco
7. The act of organizing elements of a painting into a unified whole.	**(g)** genre painting
8. Combination of actual scrap materials with objects painted into a picture.	**(h)** gouache
9. The art of painting on fresh plaster.	**(i)** triptych
10. The technique of blending light and shade in paintings.	**(j)** perspective

❷ The earliest European painters depicted animals such as wild boar and buffalo on the walls of torchlit caves. For a two-parter: (a) How old are these paintings, and (b) in what two European countries have most of such art works been found?

3 Rather than painting murals or canvases, early Greek artists often chose another medium for leaving their pictures to posterity. On what objects did they paint? (Hint: Remember the famous poem by Keats?)

4 Some of the earliest of Roman fresco figure paintings, executed about 30 B.C., are found on the walls of an elegant house called the Villa of Mysteries. As you may guess, this villa had nothing to do with Agatha Christie, but the mysteries of a Roman religious cult. Preserved as a result of a natural disaster, it is located in what famous ancient city?

5 In the sixth century the art of creating mosaic pictures reached its greatest height in the work of Byzantine artists. Their mosaics differed from the Roman ones in material. What gave these mosaics their special brightness?

6 Byzantine painting influenced Europe from 330 to 1453. What characterized the painting of this culturally advanced civilization?

7 In the thirteenth century, this innovative Italian artist began painting realistic religious pictures that seemed three-dimensional and almost sculptural beside the Byzantine-style pattern pictures of the other artists. Name him.

8 During the Middle Ages European monks produced the most important kind of medieval painting. The paintings were quite small, but filled with detail and ornamentation. What is this type of picture called?

9 Renaissance painters experimented to find new kinds of paint. A Venetian painter from a famous family of artists was the first to use pure oil paint to achieve glowing, luminous colors. Previously, painters mixed pigments with egg whites and a small amount of oil. Name this innovator.

10 The best-known painting of this fifteenth-century Italian artist is *The Birth of Venus*, which shows the goddess poised gracefully on a fluted shell. His real name was Filipepi, but the world knows him by another surname, which means "little barrel" (a reference to his oversized tummy, no doubt). Name him.

11 Who was the creative painter of fantasy, born in the Netherlands in the latter years of the Middle Ages, whose colorful canvases, filled with misshapen creatures, had a moral point, stated in a satirical way?

⑫ The most popular work of this fifteenth-sixteenth-century German artist is an engraving of a pair of hands, palms held together in prayer. Can you name the artist?

⑬ What early fifteenth-century Flemish painter, known for his glowing colors and extraordinary realism, used such details as cast-off shoes on the floor, oranges on a chest, and a small dog staring at the viewer to give his portraits realism?

⑭ Leonardo da Vinci painted very little, becoming more interested in scientific inquiry and inventions than in art. For what painting besides the *Mona Lisa* is he known, and where is it located?

⑮ Like Leonardo, the great Michelangelo was also a true Renaissance man—sculptor, architect, poet, and painter. Everyone knows he painted a colossal mural on the ceiling of the Sistine Chapel in the Vatican, but what is the subject matter of this painting?

⑯ Recently, when a Japanese television network sponsored an expensive cleaning of the mural in the Sistine Chapel, what important discovery was made about the painting?

⑰ What Renaissance artist, a contemporary of Michelangelo and Leonardo, painted huge frescoes, notably *School of Athens*, and many graceful Madonnas, always filling his works with multiple detail and carefully executed portraits, even of the smallest figures?

18 This Venetian had a long career in art and grew bolder in color during seventy years of painting. He was the first to use reclining nudes rather than the Florentine standing ones. Linking the Renaissance and Baroque periods, he completed one of his best works at age ninety-five, *Christ Crowned with Thorns*. Name him.

19 This sixteenth-century Venetian painter was a Mannerist in style, using bold brushwork, glowing colors, and dramatic contrasts between light and shade. His best works are in Venice: the immense *Paradise* at the Doge's Palace and the *Miracle of Saint Mark* at the Accademia Museum. Name him.

20 Born in Crete, he worked most of his life in Spain. His rhythmical canvases are filled with elongated figures that are balanced assymetrically. Who is he?

21 Three Italian painters, all related and all with the same last name, founded an eclectic school of painting. Their aim was to study the best characteristics of the great masters and combine them in their art works in new ways. Do you know the name of these important sixteenth-century copycats?

22 About 1590 a very young painter brought his own brand of revolutionary realism to Rome, shocking some viewers with his unorthodox interpretations of Biblical stories. Name this artist who used people from the streets and peasants as models for the religious figures in paintings such as *Conversion of Paul*, *Supper at Emmaus*, and *Calling of Saint Matthew*.

23 What is the name of the seventeenth-century school of painters that emphasized a sense of the "sublime" in nature by painting tiny human figures dwarfed by the majesty of natural settings?

24 This French painter who settled in Rome in 1624 loved the Greek and Roman myths. A typical crowded canvas of his is *Kingdom of Flora*, in which the green-clad goddess dances among persons who have been transformed into flowers. Name him.

25 What seventeenth-century Dutch painter is known for his self-portraits and his distinctive lighting of figures that emerge out of dusky shadows with a dramatic effect? Among his famous paintings are group portraits such as *The Night Watch*.

26 The motionless figures in another seventeenth-century Dutch artist's timeless, "still-life" world do not seem frozen, but very much alive in the ingeniously lighted interior scenes. One of his best-loved works is *Artist in His Studio*. Name this artist.

27 He was the first—and by far the most gifted—painter of the Rococo era. He often portrayed clowns and wandering players as well as elegant groupings of fashionably dressed eighteenth-century aristocrats (as in *Enseigne de Gersaint*). Who was this French painter?

28 Ordinary subjects such as a breakfast table or a woman returning from shopping were portrayed with great dignity by this eighteenth-century French painter. He also painted portraits of persons in rapt concentration, such as *Young Schoolmistress*. Name him.

29 The last and greatest of the sixteenth-century Belgian painters is famous for his moody landscapes that combine realism and fantasy. In his famous *Hunters in the Snow*, distant skaters on frozen ponds and peasants breaking tree limbs for firewood give life and authenticity to the painting. Who was this artist?

30 In the year 1643 countless pictures and statues were destroyed in England. The journal of a William Dowsing relates that on January 6, "We brake down 1000 pictures superstitious; I brake down 200; 3 of God the Father, 3 of Christ and the Holy Lamb." What caused this wholesale destruction of art?

31 The greatest of the Flemish painters is most respected among fellow artists for his ingenious use of color and the originality of his crowded, dramatic compositions. Art lovers know him best for his large and voluptuous women. Who is he?

32 One of the most popular paintings by the artist in the previous question depicts overweight warrior women in battle. These legendary battlers are said to have removed their right breasts so they could better handle a bow. Who were they?

33 This Flemish painter, who settled in England and was honored with a knighthood, painted portraits that were noted for the graceful air he gave to his noble sitters. His famous portrait of Charles I of England shows the king strolling, with groomsmen and a pawing horse behind him. Name him.

34 A brilliant painter of cityscapes, he is known as the recorder of Venice. Some of his best-known views are *Feast of the Ascension in Venice, Stonemason's Yard,* and *View of the City of London from Richmond House.* Name this painter.

35 The first great Spanish painter was born in Seville in 1599 and early became the court painter to Philip IV at Madrid. It is said that when painting he became an eye, recording whatever appeared before it, without comment, including sickly royal children, dwarfs, and dogs in the Spanish court. Who was he?

36 The paintings and engravings of this English artist typified the eighteenth century. His famous series of paintings, such as *The Rake's Progress* (1735) and *Marriage à la Mode* (1745), are critical of the immorality and artificiality of the period. Name him.

37 One of the joys of travel in Europe is visiting the superb art museums. Can you match these famous art galleries with the cities in which they are located?

Museum	City
1. The Uffizi Gallery	**(a)** Amsterdam
2. Galleria dell'Accademia	**(b)** Leningrad
3. Alte Pinakothek	**(c)** Madrid
4. The Louvre	**(d)** Vienna
5. Tate Gallery	**(e)** Rome
6. The Prado Museum	**(f)** Florence
7. Kunsthistorisches Museum	**(g)** London
8. The Hermitage	**(h)** Munich
9. Rijksmuseum	**(i)** Venice
10. Vatican Pinacoteca	**(j)** Paris

38 If you've seen the current Broadway musical *Les Misérables* you will appreciate this artist's romanticizing of the Paris Revolution of 1830 in a famous painting, *Liberty on the Barricades*. He used horses and lions frequently in his pictures and was inspired to paint *Death of Sardanapalus* by the English Romantic poet, Byron. Name him.

39 One of the fathers of Impressionism created a scandal with the showing of his painting *Déjeuner sur l'herbe* (Luncheon on the Grass) in 1863. It depicted two fully clothed male artists and two models (one nude and one in underclothes) in a woodland setting. Who is this well known French artist?

40 In the Art Institute of Chicago is a huge painting, executed completely in dots of primary colors, called *Sunday Afternoon on the Island of Grande Jatte*. The artist who created it was the subject of a Broadway musical called *Sunday in the Park with George*. For a two-parter: (a) give his full name, and (b) the technical term for this method of painting (which another George named Bush might want to call "a thousand points of light").

41 Which one of the Impressionist artists did a large series of paintings of Rouen Cathedral, showing it at different times of the day and year, with varying light effects and differing colors being detected in the gray stone?

42 Some painters are noted for their distinctive subject matter. Can you match the subjects on the left with the artists in the column on the right?

Subject	Artist
1. Ballet dancers and racehorses	(a) Toulouse-Lautrec
2. Views of Mont Sainte Victoire	(b) Millet
3. Parks, done in spots of color	(c) Cezanne
4. Natives of South Pacific islands	(d) Degas
5. Parisian night clubs, circuses	(e) Dali
6. Limp watches, hanging on trees	(f) Daumier
7. Highly decorated still lifes	(g) Gauguin
8. Peasants like gleaners at work	(h) Matisse
9. Savage political cartoons and paintings of the poor	(i) Ingres
10. Female nudes in settings like Egypt	(j) Seurat

❸ Can you identify the painters of the following famous pictures? (Hint: All are French artists.)

(a) *Old Clown*, a portrait of a tragic clown, outwardly happy, inwardly sad, painted by an artist who also did famous stained-glass windows.

(b) *Bathers with a Turtle*, which shows three nudes with a background of sand, sea, and sky.

(c) *Olympia*, a famous nude portrait of a model, a flower in her hair, on a bed and staring directly at the viewer. A woman servant holds a newly received bouquet of flowers.

(d) *Moulin de la Gallette*, by one of the younger Impressionists, which follows the artist's urge to paint contemporary life at its most attractive. He depicts his friends dancing in the colorful light and shade of an outdoor café.

(e) *Nude Descending a Staircase*, by a twentieth-century artist, which caused a great furor when it was first exhibited. It does not attempt to show the human body, but the type and degree of energy one emits when moving through space.

44 France's most famous primitive or "naive" artist was forty-one when he retired from his post as a customs official to devote himself to painting. Though he had an overwhelming fear of tigers, many of his paintings are of imagined jungle scenes with lions and tigers. Name him.

45 Until the age of thirty-five, he was a successful businessman who was also an amateur painter and collector of art. He gave up his prosperity to live and paint among the peasants of western France and the primitive societies of the South Pacific. Who was he?

46 From the reign of Henry VIII to the middle of the eighteenth century, all the great court painters of England came from Europe. Which two countries gave the British the following portraitists: Hans Holbein, Peter Paul Rubens, Anthony Van Dyck, Peter Lely, and Godfrey Kneller?

47 One of England's most successful portrait painters of the eighteenth century posed his subjects in the grand manner of the old masters. He never mastered the technique of preparing his colors correctly, however, and the red on the cheeks of his great ladies faded almost before the paint was dry. Name him.

48 Perhaps most famous for a portrait entitled *Blue Boy*, this artist also painted many magnificent landscapes of scenes in his native Suffolk, England. Who was he?

49 Although the works of this eccentric English painter and engraver are remarkable for their imaginative power, he is perhaps best known today for his poetry. His best works are his engravings for the *Book of Job* and his watercolors for Dante's *Divine Comedy*. Name him.

50 Between 1848 and 1880 a group of painters flourished in England who believed that much damage had been done to art after Raphael. They went back to the previously used bright colors and specialized in genre paintings and works based on literary sources. (a) What was the group called, and (b) what insect was used as a symbol on their paintings?

51 An English painter once had himself tied to a spar on the deck of a ship during a violent storm. For four hours he was buffeted by the raging wind and water, and his picture *Snowstorm* involves the viewer in the breathtaking experience. Who was this artist, regarded as the greatest of all landscape painters?

52 Commissioned to execute the official portrait of a famous English cathedral, this English landscape painter managed to represent precise architectural details while capturing an atmospheric moment. (a) Name the artist, and (b) the cathedral.

53 In the 1920s this leader in the Cubist movement was in London for an exhibition of his paintings. He was introduced to the dowager Duchess of Kent, who told him, "My granddaughter painted like that when she was nine." The painter replied, "Madame la Duchesse, when I was nine I painted like Raphael." Can you name this painter whose early works (in his blue period) were traditional in style?

54 Even though his brother was an art dealer, up until the time of his death, only one of the pictures of this great nineteenth-century Dutch artist had been sold. Ironically, his paintings now sell for millions of dollars. Name him.

55 Can you name three famous paintings by the artist in the preceding question?

56 Influenced by the intensity of the artist in the preceding question, a Norwegian artist depicted a man in great emotional stress, with the landscape writhing in response to the man's nightmarish agony. Can you name the picture and the artist?

57 A Spanish painter in the Dadaist movement developed in the 1940s a world-famous style. Learning from the works of children and primitive peoples, he used strongly colored symbols that stand for the sun, moon, plants, animals, and man. Who was he?

58 This Italian painter went to Paris at twenty-two and began painting his characteristically grave, sensitive, elongated female nudes, influenced by African sculpture. Name him.

59 After emigrating to America in 1940, this Dutch painter was able to achieve strong rhythmic effects in such works as his *Boogie-Woogie Series.* Prior to that time, under the influence of the Cubists, his works were primarily made up of vertical and horizontal lines distributed on a neutral (gray or ochre) background. Who was he?

60 Born in Switzerland in 1879, he created thousands of whimsical or grotesque pictures. Instead of starting with a preliminary idea, he began with a few splashes of color and proceeded intuitively. Name him.

61 Dropping his Impressionist style when he came into contact with *Fauvism,* this French painter is known for his festive, brightly colored pictures of streets decked with flags, sailing regattas, and racetracks filled with people. Who was he?

62 One of the most influential of all book illustrators, this English artist created a new form of depicting human figures by using decorative lines in the Art Nouveau manner. His illustrations for Oscar Wilde's controversial *Salome* are among his best-known drawings. Name him.

63 A surrealist painter from Belgium, this artist created imaginative paintings that allow the viewer to peer into areas of the subconscious. In one of his best paintings, *The Childhood of Icarus,* he shows the child who will one day fly too close to the sun on waxen wings. Name him.

❻❹ Let's see what you know about artists that are associated with periods, movements, groups, or schools. Can you match the lists of artists with the correct designations?

Artist	Designation
1. Matisse, Roualt, Modigliani, Dufy	(a) Romanticism
2. Miró, Duchamp, Crotti	(b) Baroque
3. Dali, Ernst, Tanguy, Magritte	(c) Cubism
4. Goya, Delacroix, Géricault	(d) Post-Impressionists
5. Michelangelo, Raphael, Titian	(e) Dadaism
6. Monet, Pissarro, Renoir, Degas	(f) Early Renaissance
7. Rubens, Rembrandt, Velazquez	(g) *Les Fauves*
8. Masacchio, Leonardo, Donatello	(h) High Renaissance
9. Picasso, Braque, Léger, Gris	(i) Impressionists
10. Cézanne, Gauguin, Van Gogh, Seurat	(j) Surrealism

❻❺ Here is one more chance to match famous paintings with the artists who created them.

Painting	Artist
1. *Waterlilies*	**(a)** Hogarth
2. *The Rabbi*	**(b)** Picasso
3. *Le Cheval Blanc*	**(c)** Constable
4. *Surrender in Breda*	**(d)** Chagall
5. *Anatomy Lesson of Dr. Tulp*	**(e)** Velazquez
6. *Bohemienne*	**(f)** Monet
7. *Guernica*	**(g)** Gauguin
8. *The Harlot's Progress*	**(h)** Hals
9. *The Hay Wain*	**(i)** Rembrandt
10. *Grand Canal, Venice*	**(j)** Turner

Answers

① *1(j), 2(g), 3(d), 4(h), 5(a), 6(i), 7(c), 8(e), 9(f), 10(b)*

② *(a) These cave paintings are more than 20,000 years old, (b) France and Spain. The two best-known sites are Lascaux in France and Altamira, Spain. Lascaux, in the Dordogne area of southern France, is such a popular attraction that a replica of the cave has been created to preserve the original find.*

③ *The Greeks painted pottery in a distinctive style, using black against the natural red clay of the vase. Keats wrote about a decorated urn in his famous "Ode on a Grecian Urn."*

④ *Pompeii, which was covered in a volcanic ash by an eruption of Mount Vesuvius in 79 A.D., protecting it until it was discovered and excavated in the eighteenth century.*

⑤ *Byzantine artists composed their pictures with small cubes of glass rather than marble, giving a dazzling effect from the reflected light.*

⑥ *Formal designs, with stylized figures facing front, and rich colors, especially gold, characterized the Byzantine paintings.*

⑦ *Giotto di Bondonne (1267?–1337), called simply Giotto. He filled the Arena Chapel in Padua with three tiers of frescoes depicting the life of Christ, one of the world's most enduring monuments to a great artist.*

⑧ *Illuminated manuscripts. To make copies of the Bible and other books more beautiful, the monks "illuminated" them, brightening them with pictures and ornamental decoration. The Irish manuscripts in the Trinity College Library, Dublin, are among the finest.*

⑨ *Giovanni Bellini (c. 1430–1516). In such paintings as his early* Pietà, *his* Coronation of the Virgin, *and the tender* Madonna of the Meadow, *he displayed light and color that had not been seen before.*

⑩ *Alessandro Filipepi (c. 1446–1510) adopted the name Sandro Botticelli, given to him by his elder brother.* Botticelli *means "little barrel."*

⑪ *Hieronymus Bosch (c.1450–1516). He painted* Ship of Fools, *a medieval allegory indicating mankind's immorality, and* Hell, *with its weird imagery depicting the extremity of sinfulness.*

⑫ *Albrect Dürer (1471–1528), the inventor of the etching process.*

⑬ *Jan Van Eyck (active from 1422 until his death in 1441). His pursuit of flawless reality is evident in his famous portrait* Giovanni Arnolfinia and Giovanna Cenami.

⑭ The Last Supper, *a fresco located in the refectory of the Church of Santa Maria delle Grazie, in Milan, Italy.*

⑮ *The religious subject matter included depictions of the creation of Adam, the expulsion of Adam and Eve from the Garden of Eden, and what has been called the most famous single picture in the world:* The Last Judgment.

⑯ *Because of the candle smoke and dirt that had covered the mural for centuries, it was believed that Michelangelo used dark, somber colors. The true colors were much brighter than the modern world realized.*

⑰ *Raphael (1483–1520), who has been cherished and respected over the cen-*

turies for his contributions to both painting and architecture.

⑱ *Titian (1480–1576),* also known for classical paintings such as Baccanal and Danae. *His* Woman on a Couch, *in the Uffizi Gallery in Florence, is the most voluptuous of his reclining nudes.*

⑲ *Jacopo Tintoretto (1518–94). His religious paintings,* Crucifixion *and* Last Supper, *are considered to be among the most dramatic depictions of these events.*

⑳ *Domenico Theotocopuli, called El Greco (1541–1614). Some of his paintings seem more like hallucinations than reality, e.g.,* Burial of Count Orgaz *and the famous* View of Toledo *(shown just before a thunderstorm).*

㉑ *The name was Carracci, shared by Lodovico (1555–1619), Agostino (1557–1602), and Annibale (1560–1609). Lodovico, the eldest, was the uncle to the two brothers.*

㉒ *Caravaggio (1583–1610). His portrait of the young Bacchus with bunches of grapes on his head staring brazenly at the viewer, is one of the most popular paintings at the Uffizi Gallery in Florence.*

㉓ *The Picturesque School. This type of painting continued to flourish in the eighteenth and nineteenth centuries and greatly influenced the English Romantic poets.*

㉔ *Nicholas Poussin (1594–1665), who painted from a vast knowledge of mythology. His painting* Inspiration of the Poet *is a profound statement about Apollo and the theory of art he typifies.*

㉕ *Rembrandt Van Rijn (1606–69). Tourists flock to the Rijksmuseum in Amsterdam to see the huge painting,* The Night Watch.

㉖ *Johannes Vermeer (1632–75), who is also much admired for such paintings as* Girl Reading *and* The Letter *(with original and daring interlocking shapes).*

㉗ *Antoine Watteau (1684–1721). His name was given to a fashionable, loose-fitting female dress called the "Watteau sack."*

㉘ *Jean - Baptiste - Simeon Chardin (1699–1779). His style of painting and choice of subject was closer to the Dutch than the other French painters.*

㉙ *Pieter Bruegel the Elder (c. 1525–69). He also painted peasants in lively interior scenes such as a wedding feast.*

㉚ *After Oliver Cromwell and the Puritans won the English Civil War, Parliament ordered that "idolatrous" images in churches should be defaced.*

㉛ *Peter Paul Rubens (1577–1640).*

③② *The Amazons. Their name means "breastless." Rubens's painting was titled,* The Battle of the Amazons.

③③ *Anthony Van Dyck (1599–1641). His name is given to a style of collar and beards found in his fashionable paintings.*

③④ *Giovanni Antonio Canaletto (1697–1768). Like other painters of his period, he was not quite at ease with scenes of the countryside, preferring the city instead.*

③⑤ *Diego Velasquez (1599–1660), who also did large historical paintings such as* Surrender of Breda.

③⑥ *William Hogarth (1697–1764). One of his masterpieces is* Shrimp Girl. *He also wrote an important book of art theory and criticism:* Analysis of Beauty.

③⑦ *1(f), 2(i), 3(h), 4(j), 5(g), 6(c), 7(d), 8(b), 9(a), 10(e)*

③⑧ *Ferdinand Victor Eugène Delacroix (1789–1867), the French painter who represented the Romantic spirit.*

③⑨ *Edouard Manet (1882–83). Some art critics resented the fact that Manet borrowed the design of his controversial painting from two respectable sources: Giorgione's* Concert Champêtre *and Raphael's drawing* Judgment of Paris.

④⓪ *(a) Georges Seurat (1859–91), (b) pointillism.*

④① *Claude Monet (1840–1926). He recorded the effects of light on a number of subjects in a repetitive series of works painted in the 1890's.*

④② *1(d), 2(c), 3(j), 4(g), 5(a), 6(e), 7(h), 8(b), 9(f), 10(i)*

④③ *(a) Georges Roualt (1871–1958), whose paintings have been said to have something of the quality of stained glass.*

(b) Henri Matisse (1869–1954), the father of the movement known as Fauvism, characterized by intense, pure colors, used more for decorative effect than realistic presentation.

(c) Edouard Manet (1832–83).

(d) Pierre-Auguste Renoir (1814 n 1919), who painted many works full of sunlight and the feeling of open air.

(e) Marcel Duchamp (1887 n 1968). This landmark modern picture is like a closely spaced series of "still" photographs of an action.

④④ *Henri Rousseau (1844–1910).* The Dream and The Sleeping Gypsy *are two of his most well-known works.*

④⑤ *Paul Gauguin (1848–1903). He died on the South Sea island where he had done his best work.*

㊻ *Germany and the Flanders section of Belgium. Rubens and Van Dyck were Flemish, the rest German.*

㊼ *Sir Joshua Reynolds (1723–92). Horace Walpole suggested his paintings should be paid for in annual installments, only so long as they lasted.*

㊽ *Thomas Gainsborough (1727–88). He was one of the original thirty-six members of the Royal Academy of Art.*

㊾ *William Blake (1757–1827), a poet who anticipated the Romantic Period with such volumes as* Songs of Innocence *and* Songs of Experience.

㊿ *(a) The Pre-Raphaelite Brotherhood. (b) The group used a calligraphic butterfly symbol on their paintings and included in its original group: W. Holman Hunt, J. E. Millais, D.G. Rossetti, and W.M. Rossetti.*

(51) *Joseph Mallord William Turner (1775–1851). Turner also once rode on a train during a violent rainstorm, thrusting his head out of the window to observe the engine racing through the downpour. Later, based on this experience, he created one of his most powerful paintings:* Rain, Steam, and Speed: The Great Western Railway.

(52) *(a) John Constable (1776–1837), (b) Salisbury Cathedral.*

㊳ *Pablo Picasso (1881–1973). A child prodigy, at fourteen he produced paintings of exhibition standard in the style of the Old Masters.*

㊴ *Of course, the answer is Vincent Van Gogh (1853–90). This great Dutch artist was known for his innovations in color, loading his canvases with pigment piled on pigment with a palette knife or large brush. It was in Arles, in the Provence section of France, that the fierce sun re-*

vealed to him a landscape composed entirely of primary colors. The only work sold during his lifetime was The Red Orchard, *now in the Moscow Museum of Modern Western Arts.*

⑤⑤ The Potato Eaters, The Drawbridge, The Small House of Vincent at Arles, Starry Night, A Road with Cypresses, L'Arlesienne, Self-Portrait, Portrait of Dr. Gachet, Sunflowers *(painted in many versions), and* Man with Ear Cut Off.

⑤⑥ The Cry *(sometimes translated "The Scream") is the best-known work of Edvard Munch (1863–1944). He also did a famous woodcut called* The Kiss, *in which a man and woman are fused by their mutual feelings into one form.*

⑤⑦ *Painter/engraver/ sculptor Joan Miró (1893–1983).*

⑤⑧ *Amedeo Modigliani (1884–1920). He lived a restless, tragic life among a small circle of devoted Parisian friends and died of tuberculosis.*

⑤⑨ *Piet Mondrian (1862– 1944). He died shortly after moving to America.*

⑥⓪ *Paul Klee (1879– 1940), who displayed an unmistakable undertone of tragedy in the works of his last two years, as World War II began to sweep across Europe.*

⑥ *Raoul Dufy (1877– 1953). He retained a highly decorative style which came from painters like Matisse in the Fauvist group.*

⑥ *Aubrey Beardsley (1872–98), who had a particularly strong influence on European book illustration, which began to flourish as an art form at the turn of the century.*

⑥ *René Magritte (1898– 1967), who denied that he was an early innovator of Pop Art.*

⑥ *1(g), 2(e), 3(j), 4(a), 5(h), 6(i), 7(b), 8(f), 9(c), 10(d)*

⑥ *1(f), 2(d), 3(g), 4(e), 5(i), 6(h), 7(b), 8(a), 9(c), 10(j)*

North American Painting

Painting in North America dates from the complex Indian cultures of the pre-Columbian era. Later, folk art and portraiture flourished in the American colonies, and in the eighteenth century, a number of American painters went to Europe to find fame and fortune. Not until the twentieth century did American and Mexican painters become a strong factor in the international art world, with their innovations in media and styles. You'll need to keep alert to field these questions that range from primitive artists to the present-day avant garde.

❶ In a large North American city, built 1,500 years ago but now destroyed, fresco painters decorated walls with brightly colored murals that depicted primarily gods, but also people at work and at play. These were our first painters. Do you know the ethnic group to which the first North American artists belonged and the modern name for the country they occupied? For extra credit, can you name the ancient city, called the "City of the Gods," where their murals were located?

2 In the middle of the fifteenth century, North American artists painted colorful cartoon-like pictures that reflected the violent life in the most powerful empire on the Continent. Were these artists known as (a) Olmec, (b) Toltec, or (c) Aztec?

3 Said to be the first American to have a painting shown in England, this Boston painter's first commission—other than a portrait—was to paint a dramatic picture called *Watson and the Shark*. The startling painting caused a sensation in London. Who was this painter?

4 An American portrait painter, known for putting his wealthy subjects at ease with witty conversation, moved to London and became England's most popular portraitist. He was in constant financial difficulty until he returned to America and did a portrait of George Washington in countless replicas, calling them his "$100 bills." Ironically, the painting is now reproduced on the U.S. dollar bills. Who was the artist?

5 Having no formal training, this American artist was sent abroad by a wealthy patron to study the Old Masters. He admired American Indians, and became well known for such large historical canvases as *The Death of Wolfe* and *Penn's Treaty with the Indians*. Who was he?

6 In 1531 an Indian convert to Christianity saw a vision that has persisted in Mexican religious belief and is found in many forms in the art of churches in Mexico. A shrine was erected to honor this vision of a dark-haired madonna with bronze skin, and she was later declared by papal decree protectoress of New Spain. What is she called?

7 He is well known for paintings that "fool the eye." In his most famous work, *After the Bath*, a folded piece of white linen seems to be hanging over a line to screen a nude model. When the painter's wife first saw it, she believed that it was actually a piece of her best table linen and rushed to retrieve it. Who was the artist, and what is the technical term for such paintings that appear three-dimensional?

8 In the revolutionary period of Mexican history in the early twentieth century, a unique artist-caricaturist named José Guadalupe Posada played an important part. His unusual *calaveras,* or skeleton drawings came from a tradition older than the Aztecs and expressed the Mexican view that death is a natural part of life. Can you describe the stark image that is common to all these pictures?

9 There are many outstanding art museums in the United States. Can you match the following great galleries with the cities at the right?

Museum	City
1. J. Paul Getty Museum	**(a)** Chicago, Illinois
2. Metropolitan Museum of Art	**(b)** San Francisco, California
3. Amon Carter Museum of Western Art	**(c)** Williamstown, Massachusetts
4. Ringling Museum of Art	**(d)** Fort Worth, Texas
5. Hirshorn Museum	**(e)** New York, New York
6. M.H. deYoung Museum	**(f)** Taos, New Mexico
7. Guggenheim Museum	**(g)** Malibu, California
8. Freer Gallery of Art	**(h)** Washington, D.C.
9. Museum of International Folk Art	**(i)** Sarasota, Florida
10. Sterling and Francine Clark Art Institute.	**(j)** Santa Fe, New Mexico

⑩ One of the greatest of all painters of birds was born in Haiti and came to America at the age of eighteen. Unable to have his paintings of birds published in book form in America, he found a London publisher to issue large portfolios of *The Birds of America* from 1829–37. Who was the artist?

⑪ One of the best of the American Impressionist painters had a double career as an illustrator in popular magazines and as a painter whose works were bought by museums. His subjects included city scenes: wet sidewalks and umbrellas on Fifth Avenue, Westminster Palace clothed in a fog, the shape of Notre Dame Cathedral against the sky, and the pale yellows, pinks, and greens of spring in Union Square. Name the artist.

⑫ In 1857 a lithographer and his former bookkeeper formed a partnership that was to lead to an invasion of quaint pictures into American homes. To make the drawings, watercolors and oils from which the prints were made, they employed specialists who were adept at painting trains, racehorses, and scenes of the frontier, the New England farm, or hunting and fishing. Can you name these two printmakers?

⑬ Although his portrait of the Marquis de Lafayette is well known, this artist and scientist is even more famous for inventing and perfecting one of the most important methods of communication. Who was he?

14 She is known for her Southwestern desert motifs, such as the painting *Cow's Skull*, and her large paintings of flowers. Name her.

15 Mothers, babies, and children were the chief subjects that inspired this American artist who settled in Paris in 1868.

16 In the early thirties a Mexican artist was commissioned to paint a mural at Rockefeller Center called *Man at the Crossroads of Life*. When officials discovered a sympathetic portrait of Lenin in the uncompleted painting, they removed the artist from his scaffold, paid him off, covered the offending wall, and destroyed the mural, causing an international uproar. Can you name this controversial artist?

17 Attempting to explore the nature of space, she gave new dimensions to abstract art by exploiting the visual possibilities of glass, mica, parchment, gold leaf, and plastic. Do you know her name?

18 Perhaps the best known of the nineteenth-century folk painters was an ardent Quaker preacher who painted over sixty versions of *The Peaceable Kingdom*, reflecting the prophecy in Isaiah 11:6 that "The wolf also shall dwell with the lamb, and the leopard shall lie down with the kid." Who was this painter?

19 America's outstanding painter of murals began his career in 1930 with a huge wall painting portraying his country's workers in their various occupations. Name this Missouri-born painter.

20 One of the most powerful of America's black artists did a series called *Harlem* and one called *Migration of the Negro*. His picture-narratives of the lives of Frederick Douglass, Harriet Tubman, and Toussaint L'Ouverture are told with simple directness. Do you know his name?

21 In 1932 this artist showed a group of paintings that concerned two Massachusetts Italian-American laborers who were executed in a case based on dubious evidence during a time of anti-Bolshevik hysteria. Can you give the name of this celebrated case and the American muralist who painted this series?

22 Born in Holland, this painter became an American citizen after moving to the United States at age twenty-two. After a long struggle, he had his first one-man show when he was forty-four. It brought him immediate fame. After Jackson Pollock's death, he became the leader of the Abstract-Expressionists in New York. Name him.

㉓ Growing up in a frontier region of Missouri, this painter brought a special knowledge of Indians and river people to New York, where he went to make his name as an artist. His painting *Fur Traders Descending the Missouri* (1845), depicting two men and their cat lazily floating down the river, was an immediate success. Who was the artist?

㉔ By the middle of the nineteenth century, landscapes became the principal subjects of American painters. No longer preoccupied with picturesque details, however, they began to explore the particular quality of light in the American landscape. This tendency was given a special name. Do you know it?

㉕ One of the most prolific of all twentieth-century American artists, his works included over a thousand paintings and an undisclosed number of drawings, almost all of them of New York City scenes. He concentrated on the coarse elements, often exaggerating the grossness of his subject matter. Name the artist.

㉖ In the 1920s American artists were influenced to include messages about social conflict in their paintings when they saw the controversial murals of a group of painters who called themselves the "Syndicate." In what country did the Syndicate paint their works? For extra credit, can you name two of the three members of the Syndicate?

27 A naturalist, lithographer, and watercolorist, this American painter's earliest works have been compared to the French Impressionist paintings. His *Croquet Scene*, for example, showing a group of elegantly dressed players in a sunny landscape, is similar to Monet's *Women in the Garden*. During the Civil War he sketched scenes of daily life in the camps for *Harper's Weekly*. Who was he?

28 In 1871 "Boss" Tweed and his politically corrupt Tammany gang in New York City were satirized by a political cartoonist whose biting drawings appeared in *Harper's Weekly*. He used such symbols as a potbellied boss with a moneybag for a brain. Can you name this satirist?

29 One of America's outstanding naturalist artists, he taught at the Pennsylvania Academy of Fine Arts until forced to resign in 1886 for insisting that students should paint completely nude models. His painting *Max Schmitt in a Single Scull* is a beautifully constructed scene of an athlete in a small boat, a bridge in the background. Who was the artist?

30 The last of the great high romantics in American art, he ignored the trends toward realism and naturalism, believing "The artist should fear to become the slave of detail." His masterpiece, *Jonah*, shows Jonah being tossed about in the water just before being swallowed by the whale. Who was he?

31 Early in the twentieth century, Robert Henri founded a group called "The Eight" to challenge academic art by taking a straight look at the realities of American life. The group held one memorable exhibition in 1908, and conservatives called them the Black School and the Revolutionary School. The name that eventually stuck reflected more the inelegance of their subject matter. By what name were "The Eight" eventually known?

32 At seventy-eight years old, this New England housewife, without any art training, began painting delightful snow scenes. Her works were primitive in technique, but colorful and appealing in subject matter. By 1945, when she was eighty-five, she stated that she had painted over one thousand landscapes and genre scenes. Who was this remarkable painter?

33 In 1913 the American art world changed forever with the opening of an "International Exhibition of Modern Art," showing 1,600 paintings and sculptures sponsored by a group of progressive artists who were impatient with the conservatism of the American art establishment. The reaction was riotous, drawing an estimated 250,000 visitors to the show. What is the name given to this landmark show?

34 After the exhibition of 1913, this artist determined that he would change his style completely and reduced human figures to flat-patterned forms in blocks of primary color. He gave his works unusual titles, such as one now in the Museum of Modern Art in New York: *The Rope Dancer Accompanies Herself with Her Shadows.* When he went to Paris in 1921, he was welcomed as the first American member of the Dada group. Who was he?

35 In Stockbridge, Massachusetts, is a small museum called The Old Corner House that contains fifty paintings by one of America's best-loved illustrators. His portraits of children and adults in real-life situations depicted his New England neighbors as models and appeared originally on magazine covers. Who was he?

36 Best known for his watercolors of the rugged coast of Maine, this painter brought the same expressionistic violence to his seascapes that had characterized his pictures of New York. He gave his abstract seascapes such titles as *Movement in Brown with Sun*. Who was he?

37 This American-born painter, who spent most of his career in England and France, is famous for works in which form and color are selected and simplified with exquisite care. One of his most famous pictures is a portrait displayed in the Musée D'Orsay in Paris with the somewhat impersonal title: *Arrangement in Black and Grey, No. 1*. Name the artist.

38 He used the contemporary American city as his paramount theme in his realistic paintings. In one of his best-known paintings, called *Nighthawks,* he shows three customers and a counter-man in a well-lighted New York diner. Who is the artist?

39 This twentieth-century American artist was influenced strongly by Cubism, and his subject matter, in turn, influenced the Pop Art movement. Included in his works are skyscrapers, the brilliant colors on gasoline stations, store fronts, and taxicabs, and electric signs, movies, and jazz. Can you identify this artist who usually has words in his paintings?

40 One of the most popular of all American paintings has been duplicated many times in prints and advertising. It depicts three citizens marching patriotically at the time of the American Revolution, and it conveys the determination of the citizen army to throw off the domination of the British. Can you name this famous painting? For the real trivia buffs, who was the artist?

41 Advertisers have also used countless adaptations of this famous American painting, which shows a middle-aged man and woman standing in front of a white frame house. The bald man is holding a three-tined pitchfork, and both wear serious expressions. Name the painting and the artist.

42 The most celebrated living American realist painter is beloved by both the public and the critics. His works have a dramatic quality, evoking what the photographer Henri Cartier-Bresson calls "the decisive moment." His most famous painting shows a young girl, her torso strangely twisted, looking from the tall grass toward a white house on a hill. Who is the artist, and what is the name of this well-known painting?

43 A Wyoming-born painter made a decisive break in his style in 1947 when he began to place his canvases on the floor and use his "drip" technique. He explained that he could "work from the four sides and literally be *in* the painting." Many in the art world began calling him, derisively, "Jack the Dripper." Who was the artist?

44 One of the founders of the school of Abstract Expressionism in America, this painter proved that abstract painting still has subject matter in a series of nonrepresentational works called *Elegies to the Spanish Republic.* Typically, his paintings have large, irregularly edged black shapes set against white and colored rectangles of various widths. Can you name the artist?

45 This Russian-born American painter, who was a major figure in the Abstract Expressionist movement, preferred diffuse, vaguely defined shapes that seemed to float in ambiguous space. One of his best-known works is entitled simply *Orange and Yellow*. Who was this artist?

46 One of the most famous works of this modern painter combines oil on canvas, painted board, pasted printed matter, posters, newsprint, photographs, metal, a stuffed eagle, and a pillow tied with a cord. Entitled *Canyon*, it typifies the artist's free acceptance of all kinds of real objects into his "combine-paintings." Name him.

47 Born in Georgia, he specialized in paintings of targets and the American flag. He explained that "selecting things the mind already knows . . . gave me room to work on other levels." Who was he?

48 Early in his career, while attending drawing classes at night, he painted advertising billboards while perched on scaffolds high above Times Square. One of his works is the huge mural, *F-111*, with fifty-one aluminum panels and the fuselage of a jet fighter-bomber juxtaposed with other images. Can you name him?

49 This artist in the Pop Art movement is remembered for his multiple silk screen images of cult figures like Marilyn Monroe. He also painted such consumer products as Campbell's Soup cans. Who was he?

50 Outraged alumni protested vigorously when this Mexican painter completed a mural at Dartmouth College in the early 1930s that exposed what he called the "barbarities of American civilization" in menacing shapes and strident colors. In Mexico, this painter's work had frequently centered on soldiers and revolutionaries, often painted with religious symbolism. Can you name him?

51 This rather unusual type of art was popular in America in the late 1950s and early 1960s. It is a form of Environmental Art and is linked to Pop Art. It was very much like theater, with the artists and spectators participating together. What were these "art events" called?

52 Many recent American artists are associated with periods, movements, or groups (schools). Match these lists of artists with their appropriate designations.

Artist	Group
1. Warhol, Lichtenstein, Rosenquist	**(a)** Traditional Realists
2. DeKooning, Hofmann, Tobey	**(b)** Expressionists
3. Wyeth, Sloan, Wood, Benton	**(c)** Early Abstractionists
4. Shahn, Weber, Levine, Avery	**(d)** Surrealistic Abstractists
5. O'Keeffe, Feininger, Marin, Davis	**(e)** Pop Artists

53 This American artist was born in Italy of American parents and lived mainly in England, where he died in 1925. He was much sought after by English and American society as a portraitist. One of his best-known portraits is *The Wyndham Sisters*. Can you name him?

54 In the early nineteenth century, landscape painting was considered inferior to historical paintings. Then a group of artists gained popularity by painting scenes of the Catskill Mountains of New York and the beautiful river valley adjacent to them. Can you name this school of artists? For extra credit can you name the leading artist of the group? (Hint: He was born in England and became so enamored of natural scenery from reading the English Romantic poets that he persuaded his family to emigrate to America.)

55 One of the most popular and prolific painters and printmakers in the Southwest is an American Indian. Most of his paintings are portraits of Pueblo women in native costumes, often in a mountainous or desert setting. Can you name this artist from New Mexico?

56 Comic strip characters and wrappings from bubble gum are two principal subjects for this Pop artist. He also painted satirical parodies of the works of Picasso and Mondrian. One of his best-known paintings, *Whaam!*, portrays comic-strip violence. Name him.

57 America is a sports-loving country and the artist who specialized in scenes of athletic contests was himself an excellent athlete. His best-known works powerfully depict boxers in *Stag at Sharkey's* and *Dempsey and Firpo*. Can you name the artist?

58 In 1801 this painter learned that the skeleton of a prehistoric elephant had been unearthed in Orange County, New York. He painted a large canvas of the important scene. Name the painter and the painting.

59 This American artist traveled widely, painting an incredible number of portraits of American Indians, as well as pictures of buffalo hunts and ceremonies. Can you name him?

60 Coming after the Hudson River School, he went beyond their Romantic landscapes to a remarkable synthesis of realism and spiritual intensity. In South America he painted *Heart of the Andes*, which brought him acclaim as the "first truly independent artist of the New World." Who was he?

61 A self-taught artist named Francis Guy (1760–1820) used an ingenious device in painting landscapes. When he saw a scene that pleased him, he set up a special tent with an opening, the size of his intended picture, facing the scene. The opening had a frame, enclosing a panel of stretched black gauze, on which he sketched with chalk. Can you guess how he used this device to paint landscapes?

❻❷ One of Canada's most famous artists was only forty when he drowned in a canoeing accident. He painted hundreds of landscapes and was the inspiration for a group of painters called the Group of Seven, who were important in early twentieth-century Canadian art. Who was he?

Answers

① *These were American Indians who settled in Mexico. The gleaming city of wide thoroughfares, stone and wood buildings, and huge pyramids and temples, was called Teotihuacán.*

② *(c) The Aztecs painted these cartoon-like pictures, but were best known for their giant sculptures, which are among the most important in the history of early art.*

③ *John Singleton Copley, who was born in Boston in 1738 and died in London in 1815. Watson, the wealthy London merchant who commissioned the painting, had a leg bitten off by a shark while swimming in Havana harbor. The painting shows the pale Watson being rescued from the shark.*

④ *Gilbert Stuart (1755–1828). His portraits had a straightforward realism.*

⑤ *Benjamin West, who was born in Pennsylvania in 1738 and died in London in 1820. He introduced the Neoclassical style to British painting.*

⑥ *The Virgin of Guadalupe. Even today, many pilgrims go to the shrine near Mexico City to see the Indian Juan Diego's miraculous tilma (shirt) in which he collected the out-of-season roses which the Virgin caused to bloom on the barren land.*

⑦ *Raphaelle Peale (1774–1825), the son of a well-known painter, Charles Wilson Peale (1741–1827). The special type of realism described is called* trompe-l'oeil.

⑧ *A "death's head," smiling atop a fully clothed skeleton body that is riding a horse or engaged in some other activity.*

⑨ *1(g), 2(e), 3(d), 4(i), 5(h), 6(b), 7(e), 8(h), 9(j), 10(c).*

⑩ *John James Audubon (1785–1851). He did not exactly paint "from life." He shot the birds and then painted them.*

⑪ *Childe Hassam (1859–1935) learned from Monet's techniques, but the difference in the light of Europe and of North America make his paintings less vibrant in color.*

⑫ *Nathaniel Currier (1813–88) and James M. Ives (1824–95). They published enormously popular prints, which influenced such folk artists as Grandma Moses (1860–91).*

⑬ *Samuel Finley Breese Morse (1791–1872). (Did you know he was an artist?)*

⑭ *Georgia O'Keeffe (1887—1986), who found her inspiration in the western United States.*

⑮ *Mary Cassatt (1855–1926). She was influenced by the French Impressionists, especially Degas, who invited her to exhibit with them.*

⑯ *Diego Rivera (1886–1957). He also painted a fresco in Detroit called* Detroit Industry *(1932–33) that concentrated on the industries of that city.*

⑰ *Irene Rice Pereira (1901–71). She attempted to find new forms by which the scientific revolution could be expressed.*

⑱ *The Quaker painter was Edward Hicks (1780–1849).*

⑲ *Thomas Hart Benton (1889–1975), one of the most popular of the regionalist artists. His lively canvases have become legends in paint.*

⑳ *Jacob Lawrence (1917–), the best-known of the painters in the early days of the movement for equal rights.*

㉑ *The Sacco-Vanzetti case, depicted by Ben Shahn (1898–1969). He is considered to typify the American social artist, representing social art at its most eloquent and most convincing. The pictures show the two men manacled to each other, the governor's top-hatted committee above the two coffins, and the stony face of the judge.*

㉒ *Willem de Kooning (1904–).* One of his typical abstract paintings is Woman with Bicycle.

㉓ *George Caleb Bingham (1811–79). He was also active in Missouri politics, and many of his later paintings deal with political subjects.*

㉔ *This new tendency was called "luminism."*

㉕ *Reginald Marsh (1898–1954). Born in Paris, he is remembered for such city scenes as* Why Not Use the 'L' *and* Negroes on Rockaway Beach. *He aimed to do for his modern city what William Hogarth had done for eighteenth-century London.*

㉖ *The Syndicate, which included Diego Rivera, José Orozco, and David Siqueiros, lived and painted in Mexico.*

㉗ *Winslow Homer (1836–1920), one of America's most versatile painters.*

㉘ *Thomas Nast (1840–1902), the German-American cartoonist who proved that the drawing pen can be mightier than the sword.*

㉙ *The artist, also known as a photographer, was Thomas Eakins (1844–1916).*

㉚ *Albert Pinkham Ryder (1847–1917). He wrote to the collector Thomas B. Clarke: "I am in ecstasies over my Jonah, such a lovely turmoil of boiling water and everything."*

㉛ *The "Ashcan School of Art" was the name given to these artists who dared fly in the face of convention by painting drunks and prostitutes, pushcart peddlers and coal miners, and bedrooms and barrooms. In the positive and euphoric times of Teddy Roosevelt, such a choice of subject matter caused them to be labeled socialists and anarchists.*

㉜ *Grandma Moses (1860–1961), who almost singlehandedly sparked the art world's interest in folk painting. Her famous painting* Out for the Christmas Trees *is popular on holiday greeting cards.*

㉝ *The Armory Show, now conceded to have done more to modify American taste in art than any event before or since.*

③④ *Man Ray (1890–1976), also famous as a photographer.*

③⑤ *Norman Rockwell (1894–1978). He managed to create the essence of Americana in his paintings which show dramatic moments in the lives of his subjects.*

③⑥ *John Marin (1870–1953). He said that he wanted to express in his paintings "great forces at work" and "the warring of the great and small."*

③⑦ *James McNeill Whistler (1834–1903). The popular painting* Arrangement in Black and Grey, No. 1 *is better known as* Whistler's Mother.

③⑧ *Edward Hopper (1882–1967). He stood apart from both the abstract and the Social realist tendencies of his time, painting the American environment as he saw it, but without comment.*

③⑨ *Stuart Davis (1894–1964). He explained that he used words in his paintings because they are part of the urban scene: "We see words everywhere in modern life, we're bombarded by them. But physically words are also shapes."*

④⓪ *The painting, of course, was* The Spirit of '76, *and the painter was Archibald Willard (1836–1918).*

④ *The painting* American Gothic *is the work of Grant Wood (1891–1942), who also painted a satirical portrait,* Daughters of the Revolution, *showing three tight-lipped ladies drinking tea in front of a reproduction of Leutze's* Washington Crossing the Delaware.

④ *Andrew Wyeth (1917–), the son and pupil of the well-known illustrator N.C. Wyeth. His famous painting is called* Christina's World, *one of many works using neighbors in Pennsylvania and Maine as models.*

④ *Jackson Pollock (1912–56), who was able to achieve important works of art, both dramatic and lyrical in their impact, using this technique.*

④ *Robert Motherwell (1915–91). He used what he called "naturalistic" colors, the blues of the sea and sky, the greens of trees and plants, and the browns of the earth.*

④ *Mark Rothko (1913–70), who painted increasingly tragic and somber works in his later years and committed suicide in 1970.*

④ *Robert Rauschenberg (1925–), who once said, "Painting relates to both art and life . . . I try to act in that gap between the two."*

④⑦ *Jasper Johns (1930–), who, along with Robert Rauschenberg, provided a bridge to Pop Art.*

④⑧ *James Rosenquist (1933–). His large canvas,* The Light That Won't Fail, I, *is at the Hirshorn Museum and Sculpture Garden in Washington, D.C.*

④⑨ *Andy Warhol (1926– 87). He once said, "I think it would be terrific if everybody was alike. The reason I'm painting this way is because I want to be a machine."*

⑤⓪ *José Orozco (1883– 1949), well-known for portraying the dignity and strength of the Mexican peons who fought in the various revolutions.*

⑤① *These were called "happenings." They can be defined as assemblages on the move.*

⑤② *1(e), 2(d), 3(a), 4(b), 5(c).*

⑤③ *John Singer Sargent (1856–1925), the popular artist whose works are more numerous in the museums of Paris and London than New York. He modeled his brilliant style on Velasquez, and had a sure eye for the most important features of his subjects.*

(54) *Thomas Cole (1801–48), the leading painter of the Hudson River School, which made landscapes a respected genre of painting in the United States.*

(55) *R.C. Gorman (1933–), a prolific artist whose graphics are sold to a large number of private collectors. For many years Gorman has gone to his studio to complete one painting a day, often finishing by noon.*

(56) *Roy Lichtenstein (1923–). He promises to be the Pop artist with the most lasting reputation. His famous painting* Whaam! *is owned by the prestigious Tate Gallery in London.*

(57) *George Bellows (1882–1924), one of the primary figures in the Ashcan School as well as the country's most famous painter of sports scenes.*

(58) *Charles Willson Peale (1741–1827) was the painter;* Exhuming the First American Mastodon *was the painting.*

(59) *George Caitlin (1796–1872) was the American artist obsessed with painting American Indians.*

(60) *Frederic E. Church (1826–1900), who also painted the remarkable* Rainy Season in the Tropics, *showing a luminous rainbow almost encircling the scene.*

(61) *He sketched the land-scape on the black gauze, based on what he saw through the hole, and used his sketch as the outline for the finished painting. One of his best-known works is* Winter Scene in Brooklyn.

(62) *Tom Thomson (1877–1917).*